info
The complete tra

Distributed by:

UK
A.A. Publishing
(A Division of the
Automobile Association)
Fanum House
Basingstroke
Hampshire RG21 2EA

Australia
Gordon & Gotch Ltd,
25-37 Huntingdale Road,
Burwood
Victoria 3125

tp Tourist Publications

First published and produced
in Australia in 1990 by:

T.P. Books & Print Pty Ltd
Suite 13, 3 Moore Lane
Harbord Village
Harbord NSW 2096

In Association with:

Tourist Publications
6 Pilliou Street
Koliatsou Square
112 55 Athens, Greece

© Copyright Tourist Publications 1990

Editorial Directors:	L. Starr
	Y. Skordilis
Author:	Bill Howie
Typography:	M. Roetman
Design:	C. Mills
Layout:	C. Mills
Photosetting:	Deblaere Typesetting Pty Ltd
Photographs:	Finley Holiday Films L.A.
Maps:	Judy Trim

Printed in Australia

ISBN 1 872163 40 8

All rights reserved. No part of this book may be reproduced or transmitted in any form or by any means, electronic or mechanical, including photocopying, recording or by any information storage and retrieval system, without written permission from the publisher.

Due to the wealth of information available, it has been necessary to be selective. Sufficient detail is given to allow the visitor to make choices depending on personal taste, and the information has been carefully checked. However, errors creep in and changes will occur. We hope you will forgive the errors and omissions and find this book a helpful compa

ABOUT THIS GUIDE

Los Angeles, the free to all city, the accessible to all city, the city which loves visitors.

This great metropolitan conglomerate which spreads between the hills of Southern California and the Pacific Ocean is, in fact a shrine to the new pantheon of gods: the Mustange, the Mercedes and the Maserati, 110,000 kilometres of freeways and boulevards writhe and snake through the heart and veins of Los Angeles County.

Regrettably too many visitors fly into Los Angeles and spend the required time allowed by their package holiday, they then return to the airport convinced that they have seen the wisdom that is Los Angeles, but they have not.

Walk the streets, take the local buses, with the help of this guide you can see and feel the real L.A.

Part I offers information of L.A., its history, religions, culture, geology, flora, fauna etc.

Part II explores the varied streets of L.A., and takes you on a relaxed flight into fantasy of Beverly Hills, Bel Air and the marvellous beaches.

Part III includes hints on gaining accommodation and a comprehensive list of what is available.

Part IV presents the practicalities, how to get around where to eat, best shopping, where to go for assistance and more.

Part V will be invaluable to business travellers.

Los Angeles is a city of Angels and we hope that you will enjoy everything that Los Angeles stands for.

ACKNOWLEDGEMENT

We gratefully acknowledge the help of **QANTAS Airways, The Spirit of Australia**, and in particular, **Ken Boys, Media Relations Manager of QANTAS**, for invaluable help in gaining material for this book. Similarly we are appreciative of the assistance of the **Century Plaza Hotel, Los Angeles**, and **Bob Hopper**, a guide and a friend. Our special thanks and friendly regards go also to **Marion Dillon, Associate Manager, Public Relations**, of the **Greater Los Angeles Visitors & Convention Bureau**, for her invaluable help, enthusiasm and encouragement in our project. We are similarly in debt to **James Norton, Supervisor, Editorial**, from the **Southern California Automobile Club, AAA**, for his advise, time and information.

Table of Contents

PART I - LOS ANGELES AND HER PEOPLE

- The City of Angeles 9
- Geology and Geography 11
- Climate 12
- Flora and Fauna 14
- Government 15
- Education 16
- Justice 16
- Commerce and Industry 17
- Religion 17
- People 18
- Meeting People 26
- Language 28
- Literature 29
- Theatre 31
- Music 32
- Dance 33
- Movies and Television 34
- Art 34
- Design 35
- Sport and Recreation 35
- Cuisine 37
- Mythology 37
- Historical and Cultural Dates 38
- Tourism 48

PART II - SIGHTSEEING

- LOS ANGELES 55
- DOWNTOWN 57
  - El Pueblo 57
  - Union Station 58
  - Chinatown and Little Tokyo 60
  - Lower Downtown 62
  - Biltmore Hotel 62
  - City Hall 63
  - The Garment District 63
  - Upper Downtown 64
  - Bonaventure Hotel 64
  - Music Centre 65
  - Exposition Park 66
  - Angelino Height 67
  - Echo Park 67
  - Dodger Stadium 68

HOLLYWOOD	69
KCET Studios	69
Griffith Park	69
Hollywood Park	71
Universal Studios	71
KTLA Studios	74
Gower Gulch	74
Cinerama Dome Theatre	75
Berwin Entertainment Centre	75
Hollywood and Vine	76
Pantages Theatre	77
Capitol Records	78
The Walk of Fame	78
Hollywood Wax Museum	80
Mann's Chinese Theatre	80
Yamashiro	80
The Magic Castle	81
Hollywood Bowl	82
Sunset Strip	82
Chateau Marmont	83
Rock Row	84
Melrose Avenue	86
Fairfax District	87
Wilshire Boulevard	89
BEVERLY HILLS	91
Rodeo Drive	95
Bel Air	96
Century City	97
Westwood Village	98
BEACHES	101
Santa Monica	101
Pacific Palisades	105
Malibu	107
NEARBY DISTRICTS	108, 113

PART III - ACCOMMODATION
Hotels-Motels	121

PART IV - PRACITCAL INFORMATION
A-Z Summary	136

PART V - BUSINESS GUIDE | 183

MAPS
Los Angeles	117
California	193

INDEX | 194

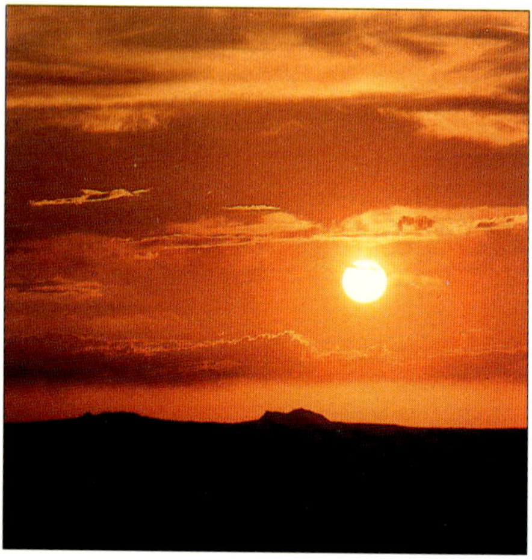

PART I
General Introduction

City Hall

LOS ANGELES & HER PEOPLE

THE CITY OF ANGELS

The J. Paul Getty Museum is one of Los Angeles' finest institutions. It is a cultural highlight in a world of glitter and hype. It is free to all. It is accessible. And, it loves visitors; well, most visitors that is, unless they are .... PEDESTRIANS!.

Because of problems with parking in the residential streets of nearby Malibu the museum's trustees have decreed that all who enter the gates of this most imposing establishment must have either a parking stub from a recognised parking lot or a bus pass to show that one has arrived by means of wheels and not by shank's pony.

Somehow this is a wonderful metaphor for everything Los Angeles apparently stands for.

Los Angeles, this great metropolitan conglomerate spread-eagled between the hills of Southern California and the Pacific ocean is, in fact, a shrine to the new pantheon of gods: the Mustang, the Mercedes and the Maserati. They are the deities of a religion that is unique, for both its high priests and its congregation are one and the same.

Its temples are moveable and the daily sacrifices of money and egos upon its chrome altars are of gargantuan proportions.

Yet, despite its widespread practice and the multitude of adherents, this is one creed where familiarity never breeds contempt. The Car is a thing of awe, never to be dismissed with a wave of a cheque-book. A constant subject of gossip, a generator of envy and an arbiter of social position the Car is the hub of day-to-day life.

The playground of these gods is 110,000 kilometres of freeways and boulevards whose fingers writhe and snake through the heart and veins of Los Angeles County.

But wait a moment! Let's not get carried away with this image of Los Angeles for the above is really a facile view of America's most awesome city.

What we forget is that behind those smoked-glass windscreens are people who are the real pulse of Los Angeles and not its cars. The latter is window-dressing; the former is the actuality.

Regrettably, for too many visitors the people of Los Angeles are a blur through the windows of a tour coach. They fly into Los Angeles, spend the required time allowed by their package holiday and then return to the airport convinced they have seen the wisdom that is Los Angeles and convinced that wisdom is a set of wheels on an interminable freeway.

Los Angeles and Her People

Southern Calif. Deserts

Los Angeles and its people reflect the Western respect for ethnic diversity. Within the 34,000 square miles of Los Angeles County are the shades and tongues of a hundred different races. They are found in such large numbers as to form separate communities that spawn colourful districts like Little Korea and Chinatown. They are to be found in lesser numbers settled quietly in the cul de sacs of Bel Air and the suburban tracts of the San Fernando Valley.

They are rich and they are poor. They live in the plush ghettoes of Beverly Hills and the sad ghettoes of Watts. They riot in East L.A. and they promenade along Venice Beach. They live and strive; and they fail and die. But nowhere else in the world does this happen with more flair than in the sunshine of Los Angeles.

So, for a start, this guide is essentially a plea to climb down from that tourist coach and to leave that hire car in the parking lot. Walk the streets and take the local buses. It won't make you an expert on Los Angeles but at least it will give you a chance to 'test the water' and get a feel of what this city is really about.

Los Angeles and Her People

GEOLOGY AND GEOGRAPHY

The name 'Los Angeles' is used with three different geographical meanings: **City of Los Angeles**, 464 square miles, population 3.4 million and the largest of the 85 cities in the County; **County of Los Angeles** which spreads to 4,083 square miles, population 8.6 million, and which takes in many of the best known cities including Hollywood, Beverly Hills and Santa Monica; and **Los Angeles Five County Area**, 34,149 square miles, population 13.6 million and which extends to Ventura County in the North, to Orange County in the South and takes in San Bernadino and Riverside on the South-Eastern side heading for Palm Springs.

The whole Los Angeles area squats in a basin between the Pacific Ocean in the West and the San Gabriel Mountains protecting it from the Mojave Desert in the East. Midway through Los Angeles County the Santa Monica Mountains slice a division line between the San Fernando Valley on the Northern side and Los Angeles 'proper' on the Southern Side. The Santa Monica's run from Malibu Beach to the outskirts of downtown throwing a protective arm around the Beverly Hills and Hollywood districts.

Geologically its foundations are literally, shaky. As part of the horse-shoe shaped rim of volcanic activity which circles the Pacific Ocean taking in California, Japan and New Zealand, the area has had an unstable past and has a less-than-rock-like future.

Los Angeles has grown philosophical about one of its better known 'attributes', the **San Andreas Fault**. The Fault is formed by two large land plates, the Pacific and the North American, stretching and straining against one another producing an instability which manifests itself in geological upheavals. This takes the form of regular minor earthquakes with a major catastrophe every 160 to 170 years (the last such disaster in Southern California being in 1857 with a 'quake measuring 8.3 on the Richter scale; in 1971 nearly 70 lives were lost when the San Fernando Valley was struck).

The city has come to live with its fear and takes a 'che sera, sera' attitude to the threat which hovers over it like a vulture from the desert regions beyond. Newly developed preventative techniques have meant a proliferation of high-rise buildings and a subway system, unthinkable twenty years ago, is now under construction.

The rumbling thermal activity from the earth's interior shaped the present day region of Los Angeles. With a continual process of change volcanic and glacial activity

Los Angeles and Her People

gradually transformed the basin which was once under water. The off-shore islands of **Santa Cruz, Santa Rosa** and **San Miguel** which were part of a chain attached to the Santa Monica Mountains separated and became divided by the ocean.

The best documentation of the changes Nature wrought is at the **La Brea Tar Pits** on **Wilshire Boulevard**, half-way between Downtown and Beverly Hills. Here are the fossilised remains of animals and birds caught in the tar which seeped up from the rich underground oil deposits over 12,000 years ago.

While Los Angeles basks in the year-round sunshine the civic fathers must often curse the cloudless skies. The county has no water supplies and must rely on catchment areas and reservoirs in the **San Gabriel Mountains** along with dams on the **Colorado river** for water and hydro-electric power. In the early days of settlement private water companies and irrigation firms struck a watery goldmine with their land claims covering major sources and pitched battles were not unknown as orchardists and farmers fought unscrupulous owners.

CLIMATE

Because of its location Los Angeles enjoys favourable climatic conditions with a couple of 'wrinkles', natural and man-made.

The Pacific Ocean sends in breezes which, most of the year, tempers the sunny conditions that prevail. While it can be cool during the winter period with light rain falling in January and February mostly the city soaks up year-round sun.

However there are aberrations. Build ups of currents and weather conditions far out in the Pacific can have unusual effects and torrential rains can fall. The city also has a reputation for the **Santa Ana** winds which whistle through the San Gabriel Mountains bringing the hot, dry, itching winds from the Mojave Desert. These winds help fan the summer bush fires that break out annually.

On still, windless days the circle of mountains trap the enormous pollution generated by the dense traffic. The smog blanketing the Basin is a particularly disconcerting sight for travellers arriving by air. Leaving the crisp, clean air of the desert behind as they cross the San Gabriel Mountains they find they are touching down into a warm, sunless haze as orange as the fruit which made the county famous. The smog is at its worst in August and September.

Los Angeles and Her People

A concerted anti-pollution campaign is underway following polls showing pollution ranks third behind crime and traffic tie-ups as the problems most concerning Angelenos. Clean-fuel cars and an attack on chemical pollutants are part of the attack on a quandary which gets worse with each new car that rolls onto a freeway.

Monthly average temperatures

Jan:	67°F	19°C
Feb:	68°F	20°C
Mar:	69°F	20°C
Apr:	71°F	22°C
May:	73°F	23°C
Jun:	78°F	25°C
Jul:	84°F	29°C
Aug:	84°F	29°C
Sep:	83°F	28°C
Oct:	79°F	26°C
Nov:	73°F	23°C
Dec:	68°F	20°C

Elephant Seals at Play

Los Angeles and Her People

FLORA AND FAUNA

The various settlements that followed in the wake of the Spanish explorers, most notably the 20th. century invasion in search of sun, oranges, oil and movies, have proved to be a two-edged sword in the natural life of the Los Angeles Basin and the surrounding mountains.

On the one hand the settlers and their successors brought irrigation and afforestation in their wake while on the other hand scaring away the wild life which retreated from the valleys back into the mountains and then further beyond as the boundaries of the county edged its way up hill and down dale.

An example is the grizzly bear which only last century could be found in the hills of Ventura country. And one has to listen hard nowadays to hear the chirp of a bird in the canyons of Downtown.

In the less developed areas of the Santa Monica you can still see the hard, gravelly terrain of the chaparral country (chaparral is a Mediterranean-type scrub form of vegetation consisting chiefly of sclerophyllous, broad-leaved, evergreen shrubs and bushes which thrive in hot, dry climates).

The mountains and plains of the valleys were primarily home to oaks, fir, spruce, alders and walnuts. Olives and other trees were transplanted from south of the border and, to add a further exotic touch, eucalypts, which love arid conditions, were imported from Australia.

Since then all kinds of foreign trees and plants have been added to the gardens of Los Angeles and flourish because of the sunshine and extensive urban irrigation. Hardy flowers like azaleas and camelias do particularly well.

Unfortunately the wild life is not so well favoured. Where deer, squirrels, coyotes and badgers once roamed ribbons of asphalt now appear and the noise and fumes of the traffic have driven the creatures back into the hills and even further with the encroaching housing developments. As well as these animals jack rabbits, gophers, beavers, racoons, skunks and wildcats inhabit the more remote regions of the surrounding mountains. Walkers still need to be careful of snakes such as the garter, kingsnake and western or prairie rattler.

Overhead in the high canyons of the Santa Monica Mountains eagles and hawks can be spotted circling and dipping on the warm air currents. Smaller 'domestic' birds like barn owls, woodpeckers, ravens, wrens and sparrows are common inland while by the ocean seagulls, shearwaters, cormorants, egrets and sandpipers can be found.

Off-shore whales and dolphins can be spotted on a

Los Angeles and Her People

seasonal basis. Seals and sea-otters frequent the more secluded beaches.

Los Angeles prides itself on its gardens, both public and private. Even in the poorest district there is a neat pride in the small patch of front garden while in the wealthier districts small fortunes are spent on landscaping, imported trees and great swathes of lawn.

Prickly Pear Cactus

GOVERNMENT

When contemplating the structure of government within the United States the average American must often wonder if there are too many chiefs and not enough Indians. Despite being the Land of the Free and the Brave the country staggers under a weight of regulatory bodies.

Los Angeles and Her People

Starting at a Federal level there is the Administration under the President plus the Congress comprising the House of Representatives and the Senate.

At State level, California has its own two houses of a Senate and an Assembly. There is a Governor heading the administration along with various executive officers including Lieutenant-Governor, Treasurer and Attorney General.

Los Angeles then produces a series of County administrations. Each city also has its own Mayor and councillors with interlocking financial and judicial systems.

These local governments have wide-ranging powers. Evidence of this can be seen when you cross the border of Los Angeles into Beverly Hills where hospitals, cemeteries, billboards and service stations are banned (obviously under the impression that residents of this exclusive city do not get ill, do not die, cannot read and can't fill their cars!).

EDUCATION

Education is the province of the California State. It is free and compulsory for all between 8 and 16. There is a mixture of public and private (or parochial) education.

There is a basic three-tiered system of primary, secondary and tertiary. Following kindergarten (optional) the child enters Elementary School before moving on to Junior High and then High School. From there College or University is the next choice.

The University of California at Los Angeles (**UCLA**) the most notable of the educational institutions on the West Coast is centred here at Westwood. In addition there is the University of Southern California, Loyola University, L.A. State College of Applied Arts and Sciences and the California Institute of Technology.

Visitors will notice a host of private 'colleges' which cover anything from law and accountancy to hair removal and dog clipping. This is private enterprise at work at both its grandest and its shonkiest.

JUSTICE

Justice in Los Angeles is on the State system which parallels the Federal role model.

The Federal court process has a Supreme Court as the ultimate appeal court plus Circuit Courts of appeal and District or Trial Courts. Their jurisdiction covers only offences under the Federal Law or Federal Constitution.

Los Angeles and Her People

The State of California has its own Supreme Court as the last court of appeal in all matters under State jurisdiction. This is backed up with a number of District, Municipal and Police Courts. In these courts judge and jury combinations hear major felonies while minor crimes e.g. drunkenness, petty larceny, etc. are dealt with by a magistrate alone. For many major crimes the suspect is arraigned before a Grand Jury which it decides if the person concerned should be indicted and then face a full trial.

COMMERCE AND INDUSTRY

Los Angeles has a booming economy with a financial base stronger than most individual countries.

In terms of employment the Business, Professional and Financial sector is the major employer covering banks, lawyers, finance companies, computer programmers and engineering services. This is followed by the Aerospace industry and Tourism.

The Tourist industry is particularly visible with major airports, show business attractions, hotels and a diverse base of subsidiary service providers e.g. restaurants, fast food outlets, tour operators, souvenir production and sales, coach and limousine hire.

Movies and television are big income earners as are automobile plants, oil wells and associated petroleum processing plants, canned fish, refrigeration machinery, clothing and textiles, oranges and cereal crops.

Religion also has proved to be a lucrative field with mainstream and 'off-Broadway' entrepreneurs finding gold hidden in the pages of the Bible.

RELIGION

There is no official religion as such in the United States although freedom of worship is guaranteed by the Constitution. Cynics may suggest Mammon is the one true faith but there is increasing evidence of a swing towards religion although the form it takes can vary from the recognised major faiths to the fringe beliefs which are promoted either with sincerity or, as is quite frequent, with an eye to the profits which can be eased out of the purses of the gullible.

Los Angeles is possibly the most conspicuously religious metropolis outside Salt Lake City. However this is not the same thing as being religious. It just means that there is more obvious evidence of worship and that it attracts more of the cult religions than any other place in the United States.

Nevertheless, because of the large Hispanic population with their solid traditions of worship together with a Black community raised with a similar sense of faith, albeit more evangelical in style, Los Angeles appears very committed to the practise of religion whether in the mainstream churches of the Catholics, the Jews, the Episcopalians, the Methodists and the Baptists or in the smaller halls and converted shop fronts of the cult practices. Yet others are content to get their weekly service from television where Sunday mornings are filled with the declamations and soul-searching of the new breed of pastoral ministers, many of whom have achieved celebrity status and, in some infamous cases, a certain notoriety.

Because of Los Angeles' glossy self-promotion as the city where every materialistic dream can come true it is easy to overlook the part religion plays in the everyday life of the city. The visitor forgets that Los Angeles, like any other city, is still basically composed of ordinary people with the same cross section of aims and beliefs.

PEOPLE

In a continent as large as the United States it is only natural there will be disparities in the ethnic make-up of individual cities but still with an underlying, basic mixture reflecting the fact that America, because of its youthful history, is an immigrant country. There is no overall, long-term, settled race which dominates the country. Unlike France with a distinct French people, Germany with a distinct German people, China with a distinct Chinese people or Britain with a distinct British people, America is a visibly diverse and still separate conglomeration of Irish, Jewish, Polish, Black, Hispanic, West Indian, Chinese, Korean, Italian, Greek and WASP (White Anglo-Saxon Protestant) with touches of just about any other nation you can think of.

In simple 'image' terms this would mean classifying New York as Irish/Jewish/Italian/Black/WASP, Chicago as Irish/Polish/Italian/Black/WASP, Boston as WASP and Dallas as J.R.Ewing.

In similar fashion one could generalise about Los Angeles as being Hispanic/Jewish/Black/WASP.

One thing that is very noticeable about Los Angeles is the establishment of distinct communities. Of course most cities have a 'Chinatown' but Los Angeles also has such a large Korean population there is a district officially known as Little Korea. The Hispanic area downtown is

Los Angeles and Her People

large and pronounced as is the Black districts around Watts and East L.A. Proponents of this separate development say it adds charm and variation to the city. Others worry that it segregates rather than integrates communities and promotes a 'ghetto' mentality.

It is easy enough to make generalisations about racism. Obviously it exists but Los Angeles, after a shameful history does appear to be getting more tolerant and better able to integrate its people than most other cities. Where division does occur it is in a social sense: wealth is the arbiter of society and the Whites and upwardly mobile Blacks have the monopoly; the Hispanics, Asians and poor Blacks are the losers and with little exception handle the worst jobs in the city whether on the factory floor or in the menial cleaning jobs in offices, homes and hotels.

Let's look at the ethnic composition of Los Angeles in an ascending order of population percentage.

American Indians

So far there has been no mention of the original American people, the Red Indians. Regrettably small numbers, active persecution in previous times and a benign neglect in recent years has resulted in this proud people, the true Americans, having no discernible impact on the social structure of the major cities.

In Los Angeles the total number of American Indians is only 92,000 or 0.68% of the total 13,600,000 population in the Five County Area. Actually the true figures would be considerably less as these statistics also include other races outside the main groupings.

The Indian is a descendant of the early immigrants who came across the land bridge that joined North America with Asia 10,000 years ago during the final cycle of the Ice Age. They found the Western Coast region with its mild climate and fertile soil ideal.

Subsequently they settled the region and developed the tribal and village system which reflected a fundamental need to establish roots rather than lead a nomadic existence.

For these ten millenia they lived in harmony with Nature and relative peace with their fellow man with the exception of inter-tribal wars and the expected incursions of predatory raiders with age-old territorial ambitions.

The arrival of the Spanish quickly changed that. What the barbarism of the Spanish soldiers failed to obliterate, the interference of the missionaries, the introduction of virulent European diseases and the subsequent coming of the 'pioneers' from the East finished off.

The remnants of the **Chumash** and **Shoshone** tribes,

Los Angeles and Her People

re-named **Gabrielinos** and **Juanenos** by the Spanish, were to live a haunted existence. In many ways this is still true and many a modern American's image of the original founders of the country has been forged by the celluloid conception of Hollywood.

Asians

In official figures Asians and Pacific Islanders are bracketed together providing 8.4% of the population or 1,142,000 residents. Los Angeles is rivalled only by Honolulu for the title of America's Asian capital. The figures encompass Chinese, Japanese, Vietnamese, Thais and small numbers of Melanesians and Polynesians.

Chinese

The were the first Asian arrivals having fled the poverty ridden regions of Southern China for the gold-boom days of Australia, Canada and California during the middle of last century.

When the gold petered out along the West Coast of North America the Chinese drifted into the rail gangs engaged in the building of the trans-continental railway. Eventually the rail links were finished and those Chinese who had not made enough money to return home settled into their various communities along the coast, concentrating on San Francisco and Los Angeles.

As Los Angeles was still a fledgling community they naturally congregated around the Downtown area with the modern-day Chinatown being that original site. This is a district bordered by Yale, Bernard, Alameda and Ord Streets and taking in North Hill St., North Broadway and North Spring Sts. It is centred north Olvera St and the El Pueblo and once took in the site of Union Station for which portion of Chinatown was demolished in 1933.

The Chinese always faced hostility from the Americans who resented their work ethos and their different ways. This hostility was manifested in numerous ways which ranged from relatively simple persecutions such as forcing the hapless Chinese to do all the servile work up to sheer violence and bashings. One of the worst incidents occurred in 1871 outside the Garnier Building on Macy Street where a dispute between two Chinese business men over a woman led to a shooting and the death of a young Western boy caught in the crossfire. Racial tensions were unleashed and a lynching mob hung 19 Chinese. This was done at the site of the current on-ramp to the Hollywood Freeway.

Los Angeles and Her People

Although many Chinese are employed in the cliche jobs in laundries and restaurants and still live in enclosed communities a vast numbers have now integrated into the general community and with their keen business sense have a sizeable hold in the financial and business scene.

A new 'wave' of Chinese immigration is under way as the wealthier businessmen from Hong Kong turn towards the United States as a haven when China takes over the Crown Colony in 1997.

If the Chinese suffered ignominiously at the hands of their fellow Americans so too did the Japanese.

Chinese New Year Dragon

Los Angeles and Her People

Japanese

Having followed the Chinese to America some fifty years later the Japanese who moved to the West Coast turned mainly to farming. Around Palos Verdes they established sizeable and well-run holdings.

In the 1920's the urban Japanese had developed an area bounded by 1st., 3rd., San Pedro and Los Angeles streets which became known as Little Tokyo. Not only was it a business district but also residential as well.

With the bombing of Pearl Harbour the world of the Japanese in the United States was to change. In a revengeful, inexcusable action the Federal authorities shipped both first and second generation Japanese, American citizens included, off to internment camps where conditions were more primitive than many gaols. This denuded Little Tokyo and outsiders moved in to take advantage of the cheap prices the residents were forced to accept for their businesses and homes.

After the end of World War II, the Japanese returned but found there was little room. Unhappy memories and the shameful treatment helped to split the otherwise united community and the Japanese/Americans scattered across the city particularly to West L.A.

Eventually Little Tokyo was re-born. Although it is less residential than previously it has found a new lease of life with a booming restaurant scene, the establishment of hotels, a Japanese/American Cultural Centre and renovated temples.

Koreans

One of the more remarkable modern influences has been that of the Koreans. After the Korean War in the Fifties an influx of Koreans started to change the look of Los Angeles, well part of it anyway.

Every arriving Korean Airlines flight into L.A. International Airport brings new immigrants. Met by compatriots they will be taken to their own Korean 'village', a stretch of Olympic Boulevard between Western and Vermont Avenues. Such has been the effect of the Koreans on this part of town, which edges the Downtown district, that maps now officially show it as 'Koreatown'.

It is quite a recent development so the area has yet to acquire that patina of charm and 'quaintness' which distinguishes places like Chinatown and Little Tokyo. Generally it is just another part of working-class Los Angeles with oriental signs. However as new buildings are erected they are taking on the Korean architectural style. As Koreatown grows the abundance of Asian grocery stores, restaurants, newspapers and offices contribute to a distinctive atmosphere.

Thais and Vietnamese

Other Asian races are represented in lesser numbers. There is a growing number of Thai and Vietnamese. The latter especially are mirroring the Korean influx with the Vietnam War producing a new phenomenon, the 'Boat People'. These unfortunate refugees are carving out new lives on most continents and a number have moved to the West Coast to settle in Los Angeles along with the more affluent middle-class Vietnamese who managed to escape with most of their wealth intact. There is no large community as such although Anaheim and Long Beach are starting to see the emergence of 'Little Saigons'.

Pacific Islanders

Almost unnoticed are the Pacific Islanders who have come from the Hawaiian Islands, American Micronesia and the Tahiti group. There are no available figures but the population would be minimal. The frenetic lifestyle and the 'colder' climate tend to repel the Polynesians and the Melanesians who never really get over their homesickness. It is not surprising many expatriates soon return to the casual, ulcer-free and warmer ambience of the islands.

Blacks

The Blacks' role in the history of Los Angeles is long and varied. The Blacks were amongst the founding families of the city and subsequent increases came with immigrants fleeing the slavery of the West, slaves themselves in the service of White masters and the eventual arrival of free men and women. Today they total 1.2 million or 8.6% of the population.

With a few exceptions their place in society duplicated the segregation of other cities in the United States. In the 1850's the infamous Fugitive Slave Act was used to deport thousands of Blacks back to the East and the growth of Black population reversed and did not expand again until after World War II.

During the 1950's the growth rate was phenomenal. However lack of opportunity and active segregation in the work place forced the newcomers into low-cost, high-density housing in the South Central and East L.A. districts

Los Angeles and Her People

Inevitably, as poverty and unemployment got worse, crime increased and police harassment followed. The first signs of the resentment the Black people felt came in 1961 with confrontations between teenagers and police in Compton and Griffith Park. As the nationwide fight for civil rights gathered momentum so did the local resentment and frustration borne of being ignored, mis-treated and underpaid. The inevitable result came during the long, hot summer of 1965 when violent riots broke out in a hitherto unknown suburb called Watts. Whether that was the turning point for the Blacks of Los Angeles is a matter for debate; what can't be refuted is the impact it made on the entrenched White authorities and those dreadful days in Watts still lurk in the memories down at City Hall.

East L.A. has maintained its reputation for violence. It is still the home of the underprivileged and has spawned in recent years, a West coast version of the frightening New York phenomenon - Gang Wars. Lower class, unemployed Whites, Blacks and Hispanics use the streets as a battleground for their tensions. East L.A. and the South Central areas are still considered no-go zones for tourists.

On the positive side, more and more Blacks are staking their claims in the professional and financial worlds and are consolidating their place in the television and movie industries.

Hispanics

This is an all-embracing name used to cover a wide cross section of the Spanish and Mexican residents of Los Angeles. This cross section would include the pure-blood descendants of the Spanish settlers, the **Mestizos** (Spanish/American, Spanish/Mexican) or 'half-breeds' (literally the word means 'mongrel'), the Mexican/Americans, the Mexicans themselves and the so-called 'wetbacks', the illegal Mexican immigrants who have fled across the border and live in constant fear of being discovered and returned to Mexico. The number of Hispanics in the five counties is estimated at 3.7 million or 27% of population.

The Hispanics settled and shaped Los Angeles. While the city often appears to be the province of the wealthy Whites who survey it from their comfortable hill-top homes in the canyons of Beverly Hills and Bel Air the true founders are those who tend those lush gardens, paint those mansions and care for those spoilt children but who live in the cramped streets and shop in the run-down stores that radiate on all sides from the Downtown district.

The Hispanic presence is marked on the whole county. Spanish is the second language of Los Angeles and its signs are seen on arrival at the airport, over the shops,

Los Angeles and Her People

factories and offices throughout the metropolis and in the very street names whether it be Pico, Figuero, Sepulveda and, the most famous of all, Rodeo.

The influence is there in the food, the culture and the climate. No wonder the Hispanics feel as though they own the city.

Whites

If ever there was a disparate group then it is this one, the largest race in Los Angeles with a population of 7.5 million or 55% of the total.

They cover every Euro/American ethnic group: Jews, Irish, Poles, Germans, Italians, Greeks, English, Dutch, White Russian and Baltic.

Dancer & Troubadours, Olvera Street

Los Angeles and Her People

The most culturally and religiously active would be the Jews. Synagogues and Jewish community centres are spread across the city. Their restaurants and deli's are famous and a stretch of Fairfax Avenue near Melrose is affectionately known as 'Kosher Canyon' for its lines of Jewish food stores.

The Jews have also been very prominent in the entertainment industry and indeed the movie business would not have got off the ground without the involvement of Jewish financiers and entrepreneurs from the East Coast.

The rest of the White community largely developed with the advent of movies which attracted daily trainloads of aspiring hopefuls who, despite the knockbacks and failures, stayed on having succumbed to the sunshine and the freer way of life. Since then others have attracted by the financial opportunities and the booming business economy.

Although the Whites are, by far, the largest race, the structure of Los Angeles ensures that the visitor is never tempted to feel part of a 'Whites Only' enclave. Los Angeles is definitely multi-cultural and it proudly shows.

MEETING PEOPLE

The Americans are a naturally gregarious, outgoing people and will readily strike up a conversation on a bus, in a supermarket queue or in a bar. This can be embarrassing for conservative Europeans who normally regard any such approach with suspicion. In most cases it is just harmless friendliness with a touch of curiosity especially when the 'victim' reveals he is a visitor. Regrettably one must exercise caution especially if the conversation leads to any form of invitation. In other words use your judgement as you would in any such situation anywhere in the world. It is a sad fact of life not everyone can be taken at face value.

When visiting friends in the home punctuality is a virtue. However, Los Angeles traffic being heavy and at times unpredictable plenty of time should be allowed for the trip. If delayed, a phone call from a street phone booth will be appreciated. All Angelenos understand the 'caught in traffic' excuse and in fact seem to take a perverse pride in their freeway snarls.

In some countries guests to a dinner party or barbecue will often take a bottle of wine as a gift for the host. this practise has not caught on in America although in an informal brunch situation the thought would be appreciated. Flowers for the hostess are always welcome.

One of the more popular methods of entertaining is The Brunch. As the word indicates it is a cross between

Los Angeles and Her People

World's Tallest Tree

breakfast and lunch and usually starts around 11 a.m. and finishes at 3 or 4 p.m. However, depending on the mood of the party, the guests compatibility and the host's willingness, The Brunch can easily extend into evening. Sundays are favourite Brunch days. The meal is usually buffet style and with the wonderful Los Angeles weather is often served by the pool. Casual clothes are necessary of the slacks and blazer variety. Scruffy jeans and sneakers are frowned upon unless one is a rock star, a film producer, extremely wealthy or a recognised eccentric.

Dinner parties are generally more formal unless specified by the host. It is wise to check if black tie is required (this is becoming increasingly rare but in the case of 'old money' the old values are still maintained).

There seems to be no distinct preference for entertaining in the home as opposed to taking guests to a restaurant. It all depends on the individual situation.

One unfortunate trend is the 'power lunch' and the 'power breakfast'. At these meals wheeling and dealing is the main dish on the menu and reflects the American preoccupation with T.C.B.- 'Taking Care of Business'.

Los Angeles and Her People

Visiting business-people should note that the wonderful practice of long, leisurely and boozy lunches which mark the European way of conducting negotiations has fallen foul of the dreaded Yuppie work ethic. Business lunches in America are brief and intense allowing the eager beavers to get back to their computer screens in case they miss a couple of points on the stock market.

Thankfully the Americans do not take a 'seen and not heard' attitude to their children. Youngsters are remarkably confident and articulate and rightfully expect to be treated as young adults and not as encumbrances. The tendency to talk down to the junior members of one's host's family should be resisted.

Most topics are fair game for discussion. However, the visitor should be especially careful of criticising certain sacred cows: The Presidency, Money, the U.S. Marines, Mark Twain, the Fourth July, the L.A. Dodgers, and James Stewart.

Don't be surprised at an American's lack of knowledge of the outside world. The media is particularly parochial in its news coverage and an ignorance of affairs outside the borders of the U.S. of A. is common.

LANGUAGE

The main language is English. However many spoken words are accented differently while the written word will look basically the same although individual spellings will be at variance with the Oxford Dictionary e.g. 'color' instead of 'colour', 'recognise' instead of 'recognize', 'gray' instead of 'grey', 'check' instead of 'cheque', 'theater' instead of 'theatre'.

Similarly, various words have different meanings or are replaced by peculiarly American phrases: a 'barbecue' is referred to as a 'cook-out'; 'railway lines' are 'tracks', 'takeaway' food is 'food to go' or 'take-out'; and, unless in West Hollywood, if you want a cigarette don't ask for a 'fag' as this is slang for a homosexual.

Accents vary as you move from state to state with the Bronx accent of New York and the Southern Drawl of the 'Good 'Ol Boys' being the hardest to understand. However, the Los Angeles accent is 'cleaner' and any difficulty experienced will be on the part of the visitor trying to be understood. Middle European, English North Country, Scottish, South African, Australian and New Zealand accents are the most difficult for Americans to interpret.

In Los Angeles Spanish is the second language due to the origins of the city and the large Hispanic population. It

Los Angeles and Her People

is both widely spoken and widely used in shop signs and billboards. Although the various ethnic centres such as Koreatown, Chinatown and Little Tokyo are dedicated cultural enclaves English is always used with visitors.

LITERATURE

The on-going history of American literature is rich, vibrant and exciting. Yet, for all the millions of words that have been written in Los Angeles, it is peculiarly bereft of any literary genre outside the forests of movie scripts. It is as though the city is quite happy to cede any literary title to its neighbour San Francisco which provides a better milieu for the aspiring, 'serious' writer.

There is only one writer which Los Angeles can justifiably claim as immortalising the city between fictional hard covers - Raymond Chandler. Chandler caught the mood and the peculiar ambience of the unreal world in which Los Angeles moved during the Thirties and Forties.

Queen Mary's Collision with HMS Curacao

Los Angeles and Her People

Hollywood Movie Premiere

Certainly Los Angeles has spawned a myriad of authors who churn out, Jackie Collins' style, lurid, glossy stories of the Hollywood set for the shelves of airport book stalls. But the settings are so interchangeable and the characters so palpably unreal these books cannot be considered as serious portrayals of Los Angeles life. The nearest we can get to an intelligent, literary portrayal of the film industry are in the works of the East Coast expatriate, F. Scott Fitzgerald.

If anything Los Angeles is a fast-food outlet when it comes to literature: easily digestible, eye-appealing, self-service words. A walk through bookstores like Brentano's will show the heavy emphasis placed on the stream of biographies (show business), light fiction and self-satisfied life-style guides to dieting, mind-expansion and sexual enrichment.

On the other hand the movies have produced a legacy of fine writing and whether this qualifies as 'literature' is up to individual definition. Even if not accepted as part of the mainstream due to the ephemeral nature of films there is every chance the scripts of people like Garson Kanin, Orson Welles, Dalton Trumbo, Billy Wilder, Neil Simon, F. Scott Fitzgerald, Paul Mazursky and Stirling Silliphant will eventually be accepted for their own worth.

THEATRE

New York is a Theatre Town; Los Angeles is a Movie Town.

That would be a general reaction when comparing the state of theatre in both cities. To give credit where credit is due, undoubtedly New York rates as the home of the best theatre in the United States; its theatrical heritage has ensured that. Nevertheless it would be unfair to dismiss Los Angeles simply because its theatre is overshadowed by the movie-making colossus.

And yet, simply because of the film business, theatre in Los Angeles has survived if only as a training ground for aspiring film actors and as a backstop when the movie parts run out.

If anything, the precarious nature of movies, gives an edge and an incentive to the actor and the theatrical scene in L. A. has always been distinguished by liveliness, innovation and risk-taking qualities which are in short supply on Broadway. A case of 'way off-Broadway'.

Possibly the first theatrical productions in America were staged here as the Spanish expeditionary fleet which came to the West Coast had several incipient actors on board who gave performances at the various missions which the Spanish established.

The real boom in theatre came after World War II. The flood of new immigrants to California included many refugees from Old World where theatre was a way of life. The attraction of Hollywood also drew increasing numbers of stardom-seekers. Inevitably new theatrical traditions were established which were encouraged by such giants as Orson Welles and John Houseman who transported across the continent the ideas and energy with which they had established the famed Mercury Theatre in New York.

Theatre today in L.A. is going through a renaissance period as the television-generation, jaded with the daily banal outpourings of the legion of TV stations in the city, re-discover, or discover for the first time, the cultural blessings of live theatre.

The venues are many and well managed. There are the larger theatres like the Schubert, the Pantages and the Dorothy Chandler Pavilion where the major Broadway musicals are staged and there are the cosy intimate theatres like the charming Westwood Playhouse, the Mayfair and the Coast Playhouse where revues, two-handers and alternative productions are produced.

Incidentally the major shows are definitely 'hot ticket' items and if possible enquire about booking seats before leaving for Los Angeles.

Los Angeles and Her People

MUSIC

Although Los Angeles has a thriving music culture of its own, once again we can see the influence of the film industry lurking in the background.

To a lesser degree, but just as enthusiastically as the actors,, musicians, conductors and composers came to the city to seek musical fame and fortune. The spin off to the musical industry outside the movies was enormous and was mirrored in the establishment of Los Angeles as the centre of record production in the world and as a city with its own symphony orchestra of world renown.

Even with the silent movies orchestras were employed on the set to provide a 'mood' for the actors mouthing their lines. The introduction of sound meant the musicians moved into their own sound studios to provide every possible type of musical accompaniment from full symphony orchestras to rock bands and jazz quartets. And when Hollywood sometimes got a fit of the 'cultures' the orchestras even appear on screen either as an integral part of the plot or in their own right as in the early days of Cinemascope when 20th. Century Fox would precede their main picture with a brief symphonic performance from their resident studio orchestra.

Although not always given the full credit, music was as much a part of creating the right atmosphere for a film as the camera work, the sets or the acting.

In addition to using the great classical masters, not to mention the traditional Broadway roster of Gershwin, Porter, Hammerstein, Rodgers and the like, Hollywood also produced its own stable of talented composers with names such as Max Steiner, Miklos Rozsa, Erich Wolfgang Korngold, Alfred Newman, Dimitri Tiomkin

Although the 'legitimate' music scene would be loathe to admit it, the popularity of films has produced a concurrent. popular interest in music bringing the delights of good music, classical or otherwise, to those who would not normally be interested.

This is one reason why the **Hollywood Bowl** is so successful. The concept of the architecture and the promotion of its concerts owes everything to Hollywood. And whereas once it played safe by offering programmes of light classics the Bowl is now the premier site for major summer symphony concerts with leading musicians and conductors vying for the chance to play their.

In turn the **Los Angeles Philharmonic Orchestra** is eagerly sought in music-loving capitals around the world. Its summer home is the Hollywood Bowl but a new summer centre is being built near its current winter home,

Los Angeles and Her People

the Dorothy Chandler Pavilion in the Music Centre.

The campus of **U.C.L.A.** is also home to aspiring musicians and also in summer, at Royce Hall, offers concerts and recitals.

The L.A. Civic Light Opera Company performs regularly at the Music Centre.

DANCE

The movies were also responsible for a strong dance scene in Los Angeles but this has lessened with the near-demise of the Hollywood Musical. However as more and more stage musicals are imported from the East dancing opportunities are on the increase again.

The city maintains the **Los Angeles Ballet** which uses the Wilshire Ebell Theatre and there are a number of small, avant garde groups connected with community cultural centres and the universities.

Music Centre at Night

Los Angeles and Her People

MOVIES AND TELEVISION

The film and television industries are the raison d'etre for Los Angeles. Not only do they help bankroll the city they also generate important export revenue for the country and act as quasi-propagandists for the American way of life (although many a sensitive bureaucrat would wish otherwise!).

In recent decades the movie business has been rationalised as it faced the challenge of television which drastically cut the audiences available. Pragmatists to a man (and the odd woman) Hollywood's moguls adapted quickly and consolidated the industry, absorbing the small, failing companies and selling off at giant profits valuable land tied up in vast back lots (such as 20th. Century Fox's sale which produced Century City). They also changed over production facilities to the business of making T.V. series and then bided their time. Movies are now big business again as television audiences look for the excitement and spectacle the small screen cannot provide.

Nevertheless the face of Hollywood has altered and the wonderfully eccentric flamboyance has gone along with the old stars who had charisma and true 'star quality', Similarly the former breed of studio bosses, ruthless, brutal, flashy but always showmen, has been replaced by the cold-eyed money men in thrall to banks rather than audiences.

However Los Angeles is still the movie capital of the world (although India actually makes more movies) and without the millions of miles of celluloid that has rolled through the gates of its cameras it would just be another city.

ART

Although there is no discernible, indigenous school of art, per se, Los Angeles can boast a number of public and private museums and art galleries.

There is a pronounced interest in paintings whether for their cultural significance or as status symbols. This is not necessarily encouraging for local artists who may have to battle against an ingrained prejudice for the works of overseas painters or those who have made names on the East Coast. Still, the private galleries, particularly, do provide showings of up and coming painters.

You will find this interest in art in the most surprising places. For example, Vickman's a wonderful 1930's restaurant on 8th. Street, servicing the workers at the

Los Angeles and Her People

nearby Produce Market, has its walls decorated with the works of local artists which are for sale along with the pastries, the pies and the milk-shakes.

An unusual aspect of art in LA is the officially sponsored murals that decorate the concrete walls of the freeway system particularly in the downtown area. On the Santa Ana Freeway near the merge with the Hollywood Freeway there is a particularly large mural dedicated to the children of the world. Other murals show the diversity of LA talent and themes. Some are distinctly odd!.

DESIGN

In a city that carefully nurtures a reputation for modern, trend-setting, it is only natural that there should be an emphasis which is almost paranoid on design. This is noticeable not only in the external architecture but also in the care lavished on interior layout and furnishings. This can be best illustrated by two examples: firstly, the plush foyers of the Century Plaza Hotel which issues its own pamphlet-guide to the art-works and statues that line its lobbies and the connecting passages joining its two main buildings. Secondly, there is the 'Blue Whale', the affectionate name given to the huge blue building on Melrose Avenue which houses the Pacific Design Centre, Los Angeles' largest complex devoted to interior design.

The visitor will also be impressed by the way even the smallest establishment will take great pains to create a different and interesting atmosphere within which to shop or eat.

While this is particularly evident in the more affluent parts of the city it is also a growing trend in the working-class suburbs where shopping centres are better designed, where shops are providing a more comfortable and more inspiring ambience and where even the average home-owner makes an effort to create a pleasing outlook.

SPORT AND RECREATION

No city is better situated than Los Angeles to provide top class sporting and recreational facilities. The wealth of the city and the year-round warm climate combine to ensure Angelenos have access to any sport. Similarly a concern with the 'body beautiful' in this city of beautiful bodies encourages very active participation and the ring of barbells can be heard in health clubs all over the city. These include the mirror-and-carpet brigade of Beverly Hills and the unpainted, basic, sweaty gyms of East L.A.

Los Angeles and Her People

Inevitably most activity centres on the beaches such as **Malibu** and **Santa Monica** within easy commuting distance of downtown and always popular with the bulk of the suburban population who flock for the swimming, surfing and sunning along the wide sands or the preening and posturing at Venice where the famous Muscle Beach attracts the pectoral freaks. The yachtsmen tend to gather further south at San Diego where the prestigious San Diego Yacht Club has its headquarters.

Riding and hiking through the Santa Monica mountains, tennis, lawn bowls, golf and fishing all attract their share of devotees.

But the real fervour is reserved for the major sports of baseball, football and basketball. Involvement is basically at high school and college level with the adults being content to be enthusiastic spectators.

Los Angeles has been unique in attracting two major clubs from other cities. The first was the transfer of the illustrious Brooklyn Dodgers from New York in 1958 who set up camp in Dodger Stadium on a hill overlooking Downtown and became the L.A. Dodgers attracting enormous support, moral and financial. In like manner the L.A. Lakers basketball team moved over from Minneapolis.

The facilities for the sports are excellent with large and well-equipped venues such as **Dodger Stadium, Pasadena Rose Bowl, Anaheim Stadium** and the **Coliseum**.

Los Angeles and Her People

CUISINE

The climate and the Los Angeles outdoor, car-oriented lifestyle influence the cuisine of the area. The concern with looking good means there is less emphasis on the heavy roast, sauces, pies, cakes and desserts of traditional American cooking.

If there is a regional speciality then it would be Mexican. The tortillas, the chili con carnes and the guacamoles are featured everywhere. Chinese, Thai and Vietnamese dishes are also popular but Korean has not taken off to any great degree.

If anything Los Angeles is the capital of fast food. Every type of cooking has been adapted to the drive-in principle of whip in and whip out.

One unfortunate trait has been the giant supermarkets' fetish with the 'eye appeal' of food displays on their shelves. The result has been the growing of fruit and vegetables and the enhancement of meat and poultry to satisfy the awful standards set down by the supermarkets. As a result visitors will find, even in top restaurants, the food looks wonderful but has a stultifying blandness of taste. This accounts for the Americans' heavy reliance on tomato ketchup at all meals!

MYTHOLOGY

The mythology of the region is the mythology of the American Indian, the descendant of the Mongoloid tribes that originally inhabited the land after the trek across the land-bridge which joined the North American continent with Asia.

California was home to a number of small, diverse tribes rather than the province of larger, unified groups. Around the Southern Californian area were tribes such as the **Cahuilla, Chumash, Hokan** and the **Pericu**. Spanish settlers gave generic names such as Juanino and Gabrielino to Indians they discovered. These tribes are believed to have come of Shoshone stock.

Further South, where present-day Mexico is situated, the tribes of the **Uto-Aztecan** race, including **Aztec, Maya, Otomi** and **Quiche** peoples, developed into a highly sophisticated nation with many variations of religious beliefs and practises.

However, common to all races, were basic tenets of faith. In all cases the pantheon of gods represented the forces of Nature. These gods could be as different in form but similar in theory as the Aztec god, **Tezcatlipoca**, the combination storm god and sun god to whom human sacrifices were made annually, or, in the case of the Pericu nation, the god **Niparaya**, the creator of heaven and earth who was able to procreate children although he had no body.

There are a host of fascinating legends such as the belief in the Sun, Moon, Stars, Evening and Morning being humans who would swim across the oceans every day arriving back at the appropriate time for the Sun to rise or the Moon to appear.

The Pericu, for instance, believed in a **Great Flood** which covered the earth and which spared only a handful who had fled to the heights of Bonsald (the comparison with the Biblical Great Flood and the saving of Noah is intriguing).

The totem pole in differing usages was an important part of the mythological process. The totem could represent the gods, ancestors or a power of Nature.

As with all Western countries the mythology of the past has no impact on the present although some American Indians would still incorporate ancient beliefs into any current creed.

HISTORICAL AND CULTURAL DATES

The history and culture of this region of California is not a long, complex one. Nevertheless there is so much detail, so many events and so many different characters involved that only a much larger work could possibly do justice to the subject. The following, therefore, is a surface-skimming project at best and should be read as a basic primer to the events, personalities and cultural developments that contributed in some way to the physical and mental growth of Southern California and thus, Los Angeles.

PRE-HISTORY

Accepting that early forms of man developed in the African continent it is believed that **Homo Erectus** moved across to China either via the Middle East and India or even up through Java. This trek took place approx. 700,000 years ago, just prior to the **First Ice Age**, with the evidence of this being remains found at **Lantian** in **Shanxi** province. The first evidence of fire being used for domestic use was also found in China. The most notable discovery was that of Peking Man unearthed in Zhoukoudian near Beijing in 1927. Peking Man, from the Middle Pleistocene era, is 450,000 to 500,000 years old. However several hundred

Los Angeles and Her People

The Rose Bowl

thousand years were to pass before the progeny of Peking Man - and the forebears of today's American Indians - crossed the land-bridge linking Asia with the North American continent at the Bering Straits. These first 'settlers' are believed to have arrived during the last Ice Age, some 40,000 years ago.

Around 33,000 B.C. oil in tar form seeped up from the bowels of the Earth around the area that is now Los Angeles forming great sticky pools where, inevitably, animals and plant life became entrapped. These fossilised remains are proof of the early life that existed here and can be seen at the **La Brea Tar Pits** on Wilshire Boulevard.

Slowly primitive American man started to consolidate his mastery of the elements. For centuries he had to be content with living on wild plants and the hunting of the bisons and mammoths that roamed the plains using whatever implements he could fashion. Eventually the use of tools developed from simple, flint knives and spears to more sophisticated farming appliances; animals were put to domestic use; the cultivation of crops increased; pagan worship took on a more cohesive shape and interaction between tribes made emerging Man aware of his social condition.

Los Angeles and Her People

EARLY SETTLEMENT
c 3000 B.C. - 1490 A.D.

At a time when the first pyramids were being build in Egypt and the wheel and the plough were being invented, the California area was literally in the 'backwoods'. By 3000 B.C. pottery was being used but this was further south mainly in Ecuador and Columbia but the Indian farmers were planting crops of squash and maize.

(Menes first pharoah of Egypt; earliest examples of Egyptian hieroglyphics; first step pyramid at Saqqara; megalithic tombs along Iberian peninsula and British Isles; Jericho founded; invention of wheel and plough; c3000 B.C.)

At some time in the 2nd. century B.C. the first real civilisation developed in North America. This was the **Olmec** tribe in Mexico. Living on the East Coast on the Gulf of Mexico the Olmecs practised jaguar-worship (not unlike the modern Angeleno!) and built massive stone temples in the jungle. Gradually the worship spread through the rest of Mexico and with it the development of earth and stone pyramids. This fascination with the pyramid shape as in ancient Egypt, with whom these people ostensibly had no visible contact, is one of the intriguing mysteries of Man's development.

From the Olmec period there are basalt sculptures still remaining which show a remarkably, sensitive style. The Olmec civilisation lasted for millennium and then disappeared as quickly and as quietly as it had arisen.

(Glass made in Mesopotamia, 1600; destruction of Minoan Crete, 1450; Egyptian Book of the Dead, 1450; Melanesians reach Fiji, 1300).

By 500 B.C. the first hieroglyphs were appearing in Mexico. This was the only significant development in the region for the next eight hundred years until the rise of the Maya civilisation which filled the void left by the disappearance of the Olmecs. The Mayas flourished from 300 A.D. to 900 A.D. during which time they constructed massive palaces and built giant pyramid temples. Astrology became popular and from it the priests developed a precise calendar. They also devised a mathematical system counting in twenties and came up with the concept of the figure nought long before it was introduced into Europe.

Six hundred years of Maya rule suddenly collapsed but

history is vague as to the reason. Foreign invasion, a peasant insurrection, famine and disease are all possible causes.

The **Toltecs** were the next civilisation, a warlike people given to violence and human sacrifices to the new gods they introduced (ironically their first sacrifices were of butterflies). The Toltec capital was **Tula** which was later destroyed by the **Aztecs**. But remaining from that culture are giant warrior statues reminiscent of the Colossi of Memnon at Luxor in Egypt. Once again we have these recurring similarities between the two cultures. The Toltecs ruled from 968 A.D. to approx. 1170 A.D. By the 14th. century **Mesoamerica** (Mexico) was to feel the full impact of the Aztec civilisation. However this was to have little if any bearing on the central part of the Pacific Coast.

HIGHLIGHTS: *c3000 B.C. Pottery and tapestry work begun.*
1150 Beginning of Olmec civilisation.
500 Hieroglyphs make first appearance.
400 Olmec civilisation vanishes.
300 A.D. Rise of Maya civilisation.
900 Collapse of Mayas.
968 Toltec tribes rule in Mexico.
1170 End of Toltec regime.
1325 Aztecs commence their rule of Mexico.

(First Olympic Games, 776 B.C.; Foundation of Rome, 753; Nebuchadnezzar builds Hanging Gardens, 580; Pythagoras, 530; First books of Old Testament, 430; Chinese Emperor Qin buried with the famous Entombed Warriors at Xian, 210; Ptolemys build temples of Horus, Isis, Edfu, 220; Hannibal's Second Punic War, 218; Archimedes killed, 211;; opening of Silk Road linking China with the West, 112; Julius Caesar invades Britain, 55; birth of Christ; first use of paper 105 A.D.; 'Diaspora', the dispersal of the Jews after a rebellion against the Romans, 132; magnetic compass in use in China, 271; Samoans colonise Tahiti, 337; Bible translated into Gothic, 350; St. Patrick lands in Ireland, 432; death of Attila the Hun, 453; Chinese astronomers make first recorded observation of Halley's Comet; bubonic plague in Europe, 542; Viking raids begin, 793; Charlemagne crowned Emperor of Rome, 800; Norse discover Ireland, 861; Alfred the Great revives learning in England, 891; Macbeth murders Duncan, 1040; William the Conqueror kills Harold at Hastings, 1066; Chartres' Cathedral begun, 1154; Marco Polo arrives in China, 1275.; Robert Bruce king of Scotland, 1306; Black death in Europe, 1348; University of Cracow founded, 1364).

EUROPEAN SETTLEMENT
1530 - 1850 A.D.

A 16th. century Spanish writer, Garcia Rodriguez Ordones de Moravia, wrote a fictional story of a wondrous island called California where a **Queen Calafia** ruled a land of women, griffins and gold.

In the 1530's when the Spanish adventurer, Hernando Cortes, conqueror of Mexico, eventually reached the peninsula strip of land on the western coast he thought he had reached this island. Just why is not clear as the tribes living here were of both sexes, the griffin was a mythical animal anyway and there was no gold. Nevertheless, he decided to call the land 'California'. For nearly a century this peninsula was considered an island separate from the North American mainland.

Officially the first European into California was Juan Rodriguez Cabrillo, a Portugese in the service of Spain, who sailed into Californian waters in 1542 anchoring in what is now Santa Monica Bay on Monday 9th October of that year.

Surprisingly nothing was officially done about this new discovery by Spain for over two hundred years despite a

World Famous L.A Sports Centre

Los Angeles and Her People

subsequent visit by Sebastian Vizcaino in 1602 during which he named Santa Catalina, San Diego and San Clemente. Sir Francis Drake had also visited the northern part of California in the Golden Hind.

In 1697 the Jesuits arrived to set up the first religious order in Baja California (Mexico). However they were expelled seventy years later when Spain fell into conflict with Rome. The Jesuits were replaced in 1767 by the Franciscans who were to have a profound effect on the luckless Indians.

Under Father Junipero Serra the Franciscans established large missions at San Diego, San Antonio, San Gabriel, San Luis Obispo and San Francisco in a seven year period from 1769 to 1776.

To work the missions the Franciscans used Indian labour either cajoling them with gifts or alternately with threats.

In 1769, fearing Russian intentions, Charles III of Spain sent Gaspardi Portola to officially occupy California on behalf of Spain.

The new Spanish military expedition combined with the religious settlements already there was eventually to decimate the Indian population. Half the Indians were to die through the introduced diseases of measles and chickenpox along with the various venereal diseases caught from the Europeans. Others died in the forced labour conditions which amounted to nothing more than slavery.

On September 4th., 1781, 44 settlers from the provinces of Sonora and Sinaloa were given their individual house lots and growing fields in an area that was named **El Pueblo de la Reina de los Angeles**, or the **Town of the Queen of the Angels**.

Spain was to have a short tenure of this section of the New World. On Sept. 27th. 1821, after much conflict, Mexico declared itself a Republic free of Spain and took control of California.

The American President, Andrew Jackson, could see the advantage of having the former Spanish colony on his Western flank as part of the Union and during the 1830's tried to buy California from Mexico for $500,000 but was rebuffed.

In 1846 the American explorer and army officer, John Fremont, together with a small band of Californian settlers tried to establish a Republic of California, taking as their symbol a grizzly bear (still the official symbol of California) whose image was drawn in blackberry juice on a rough flag.

Although this was not the cause, it was the prelude to the United States war with Mexico which broke out the same year after conflict between the two countries over the Rio Grande and the establishment of Texas.

Los Angeles and Her People

On Independence Day, July 4th. 1848, the Treaty of Guadalupe Hidalgo settled the Mexican War and California became a United States territory becoming the 31st. state in the Union in 1850.

HIGHLIGHTS: *1535 Hernando Cortes names California.*
1542 Juan Rodrigues Catrillo official 'discoverer'.
1769 Gaspardi Portola occupies in the name of Spain.
1769 San Diego mission established by Franciscans.
1776 San Francisco mission founded by Franciscans.
1776 American Declaration of Independence.
1781 Los Angeles established.
1789 George Washington 1st. President of U.S.A.
1821 Mexico a Republic; takes control of California.
1842 Gold discovered at Placeritas Canyon.
1846 Height of Gold Boom.
1846 Start of Mexican War with USA.
1848 End of Mexican War; California ceded to U.S.A.
1850 California, 31st. state in the Union.

(Portugese established at Macau, 1557 the watch invented, 1509; defeat of Spanish Armada, 1588; 'Mayflower' lands in New England, 1620; Tasman circles Australia, 1645; execution of Charles 1, 1649; Taj Mahal built, 1653; French Revolution, 1789; Great Trek by Boers, 1835; Opium War, 1839-42; Hong Kong ceded to British, 1842; Communist Manifesto stated by Marx and Engels, 1848).

THE NEW ERA. 1850 -

From the start of its statehood, California has progressed in a series of fitful jumps which would show a rather uneven but upward line on a graph.

Gold, Oranges, Oil and Films have all produced their own individual boom periods for California and for Los Angeles in particular.

Gold was actually found in 1842, while the state was still under the control of Mexico. The find was made at Placeritas Canyon in the San Fernando Valley when Francisco Lopez unearthed a nugget of gold while digging for onions. The boom period got under way in earnest several years later and the magnet of the yellow metal drew in adventurers and fortune seekers on long, dangerous treks across America and from overseas. By 1854 the boom was over and the strain on the economy of the huge numbers of immigrants prompted the notorious '**Greaser Law**' of 1855 which levied a monthly tax of $20 on 'foreigners'. This discriminated against the Hispanics and Indians and was used as a pretext for action by racist vigilantes.

Los Angeles and Her People

In 1873 several orange trees were shipped across from the Department of Agriculture in Washington D.C. and were the foundation for a new explosion of interest in the fledgling Los Angeles. With the completion of the transcontinental railway line in 1869 and the subsequent feeder line from San Francisco to Los Angeles, the Easterners suddenly had an easy and safe way to travel to the West Coast. Attracted by the fanciful pictures painted of the vast orange orchards and the continual sunshine, they flocked in their thousands to the Pacific.

And still Lady Luck shone like the Californian sun. This time one of her richest jewels was unearthed. In 1892 Edward L. Doheny discovered oil on land that is now **Westlake Park**. This dragged in the new breed of prospectors as well as established businessmen. Business received a further fillip with the San Francisco Fire and earthquake of 1906 when many businesses decided to move south because of the danger.

In 1902 the Pacific Electric Railway was formed and provided regular day trips from the downtown area to what is now **Beverly Hills**. The tracks can still be seen running alongside Santa Monica Boulevard through Beverly Hills and Century City.

By 1908 peep-shows were popular. These soon blossomed into silent pictures with New York movie makers moving to California for the sunshine needed for the early pictures which were mainly filmed outdoors. Talkies were next and the rest is celluloid history.

Los Angeles and Her People

Friendship knot, Little Tokyo

On the industrial front, following the first glider flight at San Diego in 1883, the **Lockheed Brothers** had set up business followed by Donald W. Douglas who had built his first plane behind his Santa Monica barber shop. This was the foundation of the Californian aviation industry which was to receive a boost in World War I which saw for the first time the use of the airplane in war.

At times, though, it looked as if Los Angeles would be unable to sustain its rapid growth due to the problem of water supply. In 1913 there were riots and bombings when residents found they would have to pay high premiums for the water that had to be piped through the eastern hills at the rear of the city. Private companies also took the opportunity to cash in and it took a decade before the water supply was sorted out and came under city control. Although the intervening years have strengthened the supply of water, Los Angeles is still not worry-free when it comes to a continuing supply and even today Angelenos are exhorted to conserve water.

Los Angeles survived a new influx of immigrants in 1929, the '**Dust Bowlers**', the bankrupt farmers and their families who fled the worst ever modern drought in the Mid-West which left their arable farms virtual deserts.

Los Angeles and Her People

1932 brought the Olympic Games to America for the second time when Los Angeles was chosen as the site for the most spectacular Games to that time, a feat the city repeated in 1984.

World War II provided a less inspiring chapter in the L.A. story when an over-reaction in the wake of Pearl Harbour saw the internment of over 100,000 Japanese in California with the bulk being American/Japanese with full citizenship.

Since the War, Los Angeles has undergone a further film industry success story followed by a brief slump with the advent of television which soon found a new home for itself amidst the old film studios.

Business and Industry liked the relaxed climate and the relaxed atmosphere created by enlightened administrations such as that of former Governor Ronald Reagan who actively, and through tax benefits, encouraged companies to put down roots in California, with Los Angeles being particularly attractive.

Los Angeles is in a continual state of growth with skylines that change so rapidly that those returning after any lengthy absence could well wonder if they had come to the right city.

New building techniques have conquered the earthquake problem (although that is still to be put to the ultimate test) and high-rise buildings, unthinkable in the 1950s, reach for the clouds. Also the much-needed subway system is finally under construction.

Now one can only speculate whether the coming decades will prove to be as exciting and as filled with drama as the years since the first coming of man to these shores by the Pacific.

HIGHLIGHTS: *1855 'Greaser' Law taxes foreigners.*
1869 First transcontinental railway finished.
1873 First orange trees arrive in California.
1876 Feeder rail line from S.F. to L.A.
1892 Oil discovered at Westlake Park.
1902 Pacific Electric Railway founded.
1907 Boggs & Persons start first movie studio.
1912 Beverly Hills Hotel opened.
1916 Lockheed Bros. set up operation.
1929 Dust Bowl immigrants arrive.
1932 L.A. Olympics at Coliseum.
1940 First freeway (Pasadena) opened.
1942 Internment of American/Japanese.
1965 Watts riots.
1968 Robert Kennedy assassinated L.A.
1984 L.A.'s second Olympic Games.

Los Angeles and Her People

Wright Brothers' flight, 1903; World War I, 1914-18; League of Nations established, 1920; Wall St. crash, 1929; Hitler made Chancellor of Germany, 1933; Spanish Civil War begins, 1936; World War 11 1939-45; Declaration of People's Republic of China, 1949; death of Stalin, 1953; building of Berlin Wall, 1961; Yuri Gagarin, first man in space, 1961, John F. Kennedy assassinated, 1963; Cultural Revolution, 1966; Nixon visits China, 1972; U.S. withdraws from Vietnam, 1973; Watergate, 1974; Beijing massacre, 1989)

TOURISM

It is doubtful if any city is so geared to the tourist as Los Angeles. As it has always played host to a transient population this is understandable.

As seen above, Tourism is the third largest employer and covers the full spectrum of services and attractions.

From the moment of arrival at the Los Angeles International Airport the visitor is plunged into the well-organised world of tourism.

The bewildering array of shuttle buses, tourist coaches, taxis and stretch limousines is the first indication of how well the city caters for the traveller despite its limitations of size and its lack of a highly-developed urban public transport system.

Hotels and restaurants offer the largest possible range of services and prices. While one will pay top dollar for a room at hotels like the Century Plaza or the Beverly Wilshire other charges in coffee shops and hotel dining rooms can be quite reasonable.

As Americans are big eaters, overseas visitors will often be surprised at the size of meals or even a plain sandwich. The range of deli's and fast food outlets provide inexpensive and satisfying meals.

Most holiday-makers come here for the glamour of Hollywood and the adult's playground, Disneyland. Numerous tour operators offer a range of day and night tours exploring the sights of Tinsel Town, the stars' homes and the various film and television studios. Prices are reasonable but the tours are often too well organised when the tour guide is either a budding or a failed actor. Actually, for the extra money involved, it is well worth investing in the hire of specialised, personal guides such as Bob 'Your Host to L.A.' Hopper (818) 504 0042. Bob knows Los Angeles down to the last detail and can show you the proper way to enjoy Los Angeles and see the sights that are off the normal tourist route.

Los Angeles and Her People

The car rental scene is equally active and bargains abound (it is wise for overseas visitors to check the special deals available with airline ticket and package holiday purchases).

Promptness and courtesy are the keywords of the tourist industry in Los Angeles. Indeed they apply to most of the service industries. Visitors, especially from outside the United States, will be surprised at the natural good manners of Angelenos.

Marineland

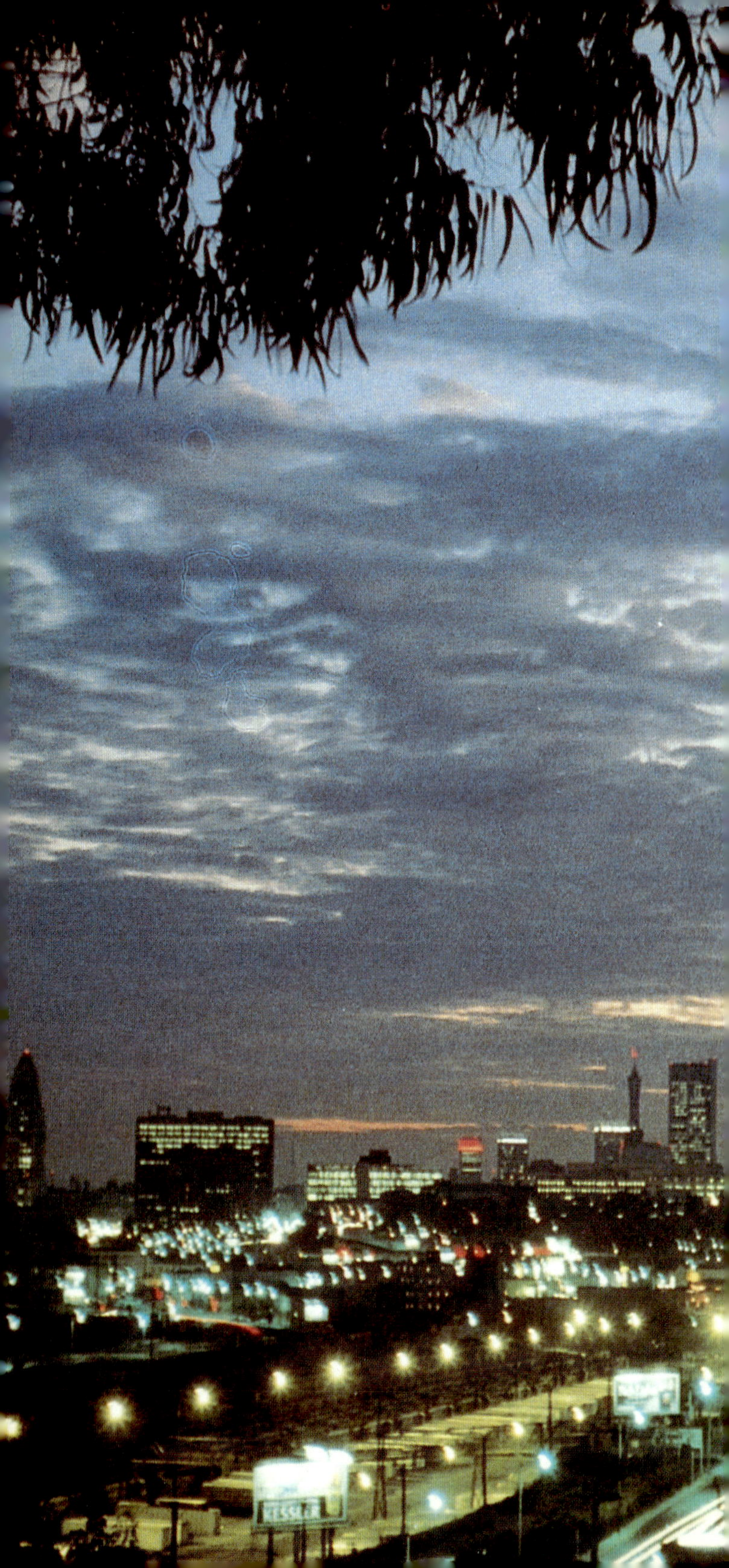

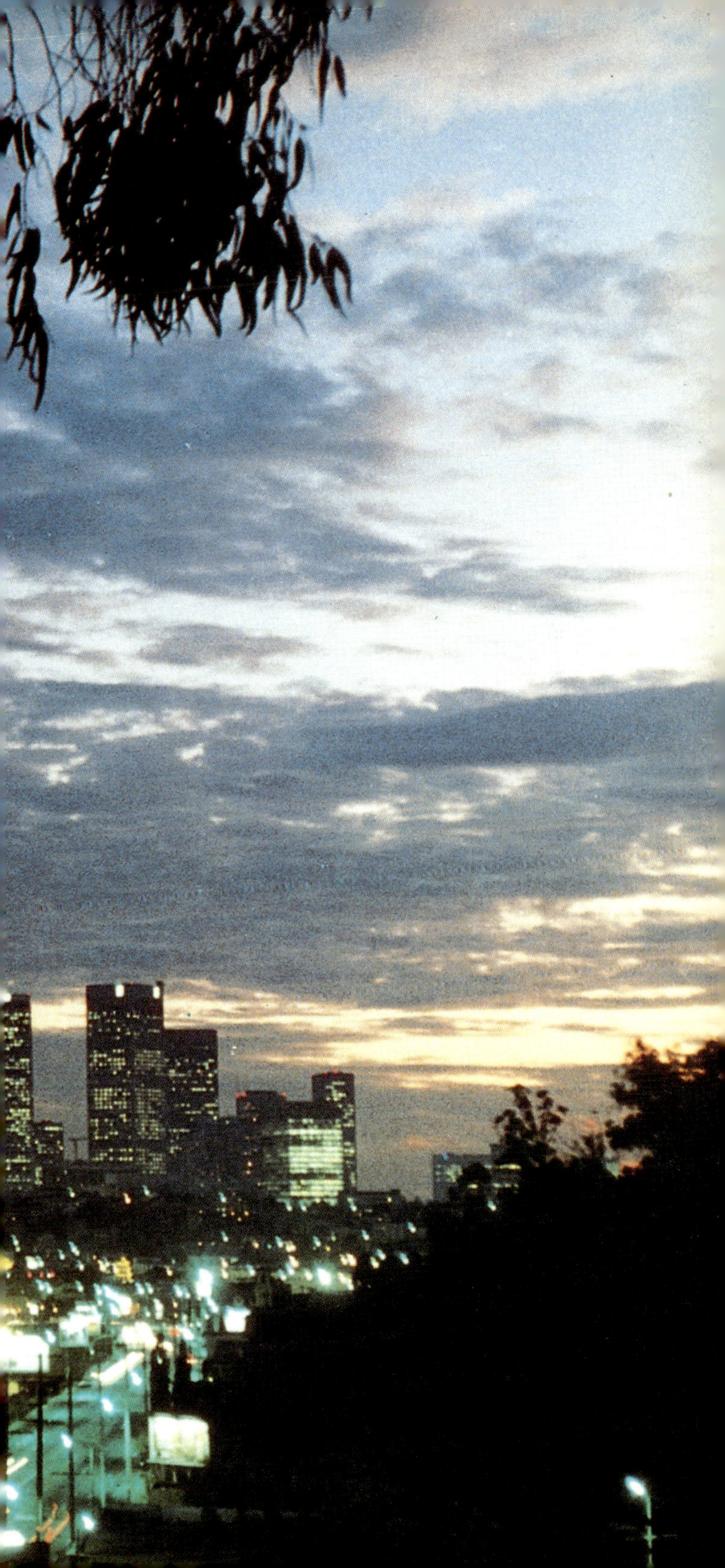

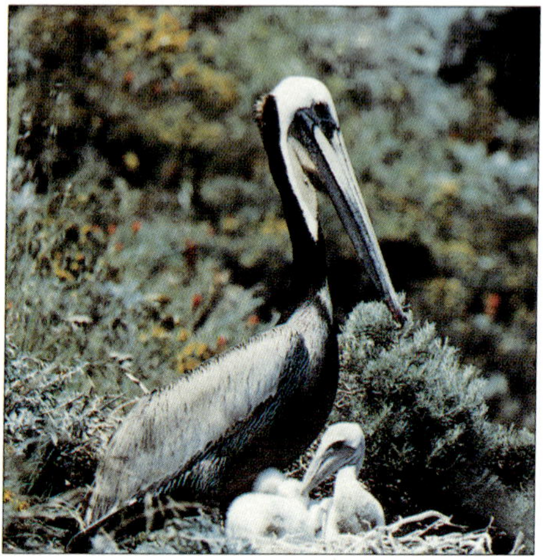

PART II
Sightseeing

Fantasyland

LOS ANGELES

For the first-time visitor to Los Angeles the idea of exploring this fascinating but awesome city presents seemingly impossible problems.

Fearsome myths abound about drivers who get onto the infamous freeways and never get off again, doomed to spend their eternity vainly seeking the off-ramp. Alternately there is the prospect of being wiped out in the daily shoot-outs on Sunset Boulevard, being kidnapped in Beverly Hills and sold into the White Slave Trade in Tijuana or eaten by sharks that spring from the sea onto the sands of Venice Beach. Admittedly all delicious fantasies but hardly what Los Angeles is really all about.

Nevertheless Los Angeles does produce a formidable image if only because of its size. It seems temptingly easy to spend your few days in L.A. just taking one coach tour after another and not spending any time feeling the pavement under feet and getting the 'smell' of the city.

The secret of enjoying Los Angeles is to nibble one's way through its crust rather than trying to take large chunks. Select an area, concentrate on what it has to offer and spend a day or two just exploring, browsing and getting to know that one section.

Unfortunately most package holidays don't allow time for that method and you will find yourself condemned to the scheduled treadmill of coach tours to Disneyland, Hollywood, Beverly Hills and The Homes of The Stars.

By all means take one of these tours to orientate yourself to the city and then, if time permits, discard the fixed itinerary and strike out on your own.

Because Los Angeles is so geared towards the car and the region covers such large distances a rental car is the best method for getting quickly around the city. Competition ensures that the prices for rental cars are inexpensive and often your airline ticket will get you additional deals.

> **INFOTIP:** In the absence of a subway (still under construction) the RTD (Rapid Transport District) buses provide efficient, quick, frequent and inexpensive transport around most areas of Los Angeles.

However, despite the lack of a thoroughly integrated urban transport system (a subway is in the first stages of construction), one can still travel the Greater Los Angeles

Los Angeles

Area cheaply and efficiently on the RTD bus system. RTD buses cover the major areas and are complemented Downtown by the DASH bus which services the Downtown area. Suburbs such as Santa Monica also have their own buses. Hotel concierges have details of times and fares (very cheap, with transfers between buses available; but correct change is required at all times).

Don't be afraid to walk even if it seems a little strange being the only person on the pavement (you don't have B.O., it's just the fact that locals travel everywhere by car). You will have no problems in the major areas however don't be foolish, stick to the popular districts (avoid East L.A., South Central L.A. and certain sections of Downtown below Main Street). Alleyways, industrial sites and the remote corners of parks should also be avoided and walking after-dark, as in any city, is not recommended.

For the purposes of this guide we have taken a rough east/west axis of the city from the Downtown area to the Beach.

A glance at a map will show that these two areas are linked by several major boulevards: Sunset, Santa Monica and Wilshire.

Our sightseeing sections are based along Sunset Boulevard for the simple reason it starts within a block or two of the historic El Pueblo district where Los Angeles began and continues through the most popular parts of the city, Hollywood, Beverly Hills and Westwood, before ending at the beach at Pacific Palisades. Sunset Boulevard presents a good cross-section of Los Angeles from the cheap and tawdry to the expensive and tawdry.

However Sunset Boulevard is only a base to work from as it will be necessary to divert along other streets to cover all the important sights nearby and then extend into the suburbs beyond the Santa Monica Mountains to the San Fernando Valley to the north of Los Angeles County and, in the other direction, south to Anaheim, Long Beach and Newport.

INFOTIP: If an asthmatic or with other breathing problems avoid L.A. in high summer. Smog gets trapped by the Santa Monica mountains and the lack of winds and lies like a blanket over the area. Active measures introduced by the City of L.A. are starting to take effect but the city has still a long way to go.

Downtown

Covering Central Business District, El Pueblo, Olvera St., Chinatown, Little Tokyo, Union Station, Dorothy Chandler Pavilion, Dodger Stadium, Angelino Heights, Echo Park, Griffith Park, Exposition Park.

The Downtown district has all that is good and bad about Los Angeles. There is wealth and poverty, growth and decay, excitement and indifference, history and the ephemeral. It can all be found in this urban island surrounded by a sea of freeways.

The freeway system provides an effective border for the Downtown district with the **Harbor Freeway** along the **Western** edge, the **Santa Ana** on the Northern side and the **Santa Monica** curling in from the South to fill up the gaps.

Effectively the area can be classified as **New, Old** and **Very Old**. It is the latter which is the most important because this is where the very roots of the city are buried.

> **INFOTIP:** Although the phrase 'have a nice day' has become something of a cliche visitors will still be impressed by the sincerity with which it is delivered. L.A. has some of the best and friendliest service of any city in the world.

El Pueblo

The official name is **'El Pueblo de Los Angelos State Historical Park'**. Pueblo is the Spanish word for 'town' and was the name given to the fledgling settlement when officially settled in 1781.

The term 'Park' is rather a capricious title as there is precious little parkland in the 44 acres of land bounded by **Alameda, Arcadia, Spring** and **Macy** streets at the North/East corner of the Downtown district.

The heart of El Pueblo is **Olvera Street**, a one-block length between Macy and Arcadia St. It is a pedestrian mall so you won't be bothered by traffic. The pathway down the centre of Olvera actually follows the route of the 1783 channel which carried water into the tiny village from the Los Angeles River. Although much of the Olvera Street complex is a 1930 re-construction of a typical Mexican market street, the retention of some the older buildings and the sympathetic restoration work gives the mall an individual atmosphere and even the Mexicans find it a

Downtown

nostalgic reminder of home. They flock here on Sundays after church with the kiddies in their finest attire adding a festive Mexican touch in the shadows of high-rise, modern Los Angeles.

About half-way along, on the left hand side heading towards Arcadia St, is the **Avila Adobe** the oldest building still standing in the city. The original walls date from 1818 when they were erected by a former mayor of the town, Don Francisco Avila. Now it is a small museum.

The walking here is very pleasant with the grape vines hanging from the roofs and charming cafes where one can get a cup of coffee and a broad Mexican smile while listening to the strolling mariachi players. A local treat worth trying are the twists of a deep fried doughnut mixture called churros. They are made fresh at a small pastry stall here.

At its Arcadia St end, Olvera opens out into a broad square of olive trees and flagstones. This area is always busy not only with tourists but with those waiting to see the Mexican consul who appropriately has his office in a corner building of this historic section. Surprisingly, the church in a prominent position nearby is not Catholic, as one would expect, but Methodist.

A note for those coming by car, the car park on Alameda St. is small and is full by early morning. Most of the metered spots will be taken so be prepared for a walk.

On Mexican Independence Day (Sept 16th) Olvera St. becomes the focus of Mexican nationalism and high spirits and those lucky enough to be there at that time recommend the experience.

Do try and make the effort to visit El Pueblo it is worth the journey. Incidentally not many coach tours feature it on their itineraries.

Union Station

A very familiar building is just across Alameda St from El Pueblo. It is the Spanish Mission style Union Station the sight of which will instantly evoke memories of a host of old movies and the Los Angeles Raymond Chandler so moodily described.

When built in 1939 it was to become the last major railway terminal constructed in America. During the glamour days of films during the 1940's and 1950's, before the plane took over, the arrival of the Super Chief into Union Station with the newest star from Broadway was a major event.

Downtown

The terminal became a star in its own right with the 1950 movie 'Union Station' starring William Holden. Much of the location work was shot in the station itself although the setting was supposed to be Chicago. Apart from being used for many other films it was also chosen to represent a 21st. century police station for Blade Runner because, as director Ridley Scott said, it had 'neo-Fascist architecture'.

As Los Angeles is not a major rail intersection, being basically a feeder line from San Francisco, the vast interior is really wasted nowadays. But it is worth walking across the road to see for its broad, marble floors, tall ceilings and the pew-like waiting room seats.

Downtown and Freeways

Downtown

Chinatown and Little Tokyo

Using El Pueblo as a pivotal point these two old and important ethnic areas would be as diagonal opposites on the axis: Chinatown to the North and Little Tokyo to the South. If you follow **Broadway** past **City Hall** and continue North it will take you through the heart of Chinatown.

The Chinese community once occupied a larger slice of the city but lost many of their holdings when Union Station was built on their land.

Today the **Chinatown** area is relatively small being home to 15,000 Chinese and Vietnamese residents but serving as the cultural centre for the bulk of the Chinese population scattered through the southern regions.

Basically it is similar to its counterparts in other American cities offering a range of restaurants supplying bland Cantonese cuisine, spicy Sichuan dishes or the intricately prepared Peking Duck. Imported herbs and spices are on sale plus those inevitable 'Willow Pattern' plates and saucers.

In the opposite direction, moving towards the city proper, is **Little Tokyo**, still basically occupying the same land which the new Japanese arrivals farmed 100 years ago.

Downtown

Dominating Little Tokyo is the Japanese American Cultural and Community Centre which provides important cultural activities for the whole Los Angeles community. There is a large theatre, an elegant gallery, a library and a **Garden of the Clear Stream** featuring traditional Japanese horticulture.

The streets in the district have several interesting 19th. century buildings while the **Nishi Hongwangi Buddhist Temple** looks older than its 1925 origins.

Needless to say some of the best Japanese restaurants are to be found in Little Tokyo.

From Little Tokyo it is a few blocks, diagonally South/West to the centre of Los Angeles proper.

This central Downtown area is roughly divided into two sections: the Lower or older shopping district; and the Upper, modern financial heart. A good demarcation point between the two is the Biltmore Hotel occupying most of the block between **Grand Avenue** and **Olive St**. In fact there is a distinct and noticeable visual difference in the make-up of the city at this point. Let's look at the lower portion first and then move to the higher or upper part of Downtown.

Chinatown at Night

Downtown

Lower Downtown

What this section of Los Angeles loses in the way of style and wealth it makes up for in interest and life. The money may be generated in the Upper district but the administration of the city is centred down here. And those visitors interested in the architectural history of a city will find there are some rich pickings to be found.

Biltmore Hotel

An official Historic Landmark, the Biltmore is a splendid evocation of a more gracious era and thankfully is still providing accommodation in the grand old style.

Designed by the same architects who built the Waldorf Astoria in New York (Schultze & Weaver), the 1000 rooms were opened in 1923. The guest rooms and the public rooms are of a generous nature and the lobbies with their vast ceilings, fretwork, marble staircases and ornate Spanish balustrades are imposing without being daunting.

It's not surprising that the Biltmore has been a favourite setting for moviemakers and its credits include films and television shows ranging from The Last Tycoon to Dynasty.

It was in the hotel's Crystal Ballroom that the Academy of Motion Picture Arts and Sciences was inaugurated in May 1927 at a dinner where MGM art director Cedric Gibbons did a sketch on a napkin of a small figure which was christened 'Oscar' and was to become the symbol of the Academy Awards.

The Biltmore fronts onto **Pershing Square**, a welcome piece of greenery amidst the concrete and occupying a whole city block. Restoration work to restore the beauty of the original park has been undertaken.

Continuing down 5th St from the Biltmore. you are soon in the general shopping area surrounded by blocks of old office buildings and hotels which, like their patrons, have seen better days. Several blocks further on is **Parker Centre**, home of the Los Angeles Police Department, which takes up a fair chunk of land. However it is not wise to venture beyond this point as you would be heading into Skid Row territory. It is best to turn North/East up Broadway, a busy commercial street which runs past the **Grand Central Market**, a crowded, under-cover marketplace for the people of Los Angeles. It is bright, noisy and overflowing with fresh produce and exotic foods. Fast food stalls of better-than-average quality are everywhere.

A little further East is the immediately recognisable tower of City Hall on N. Spring St.

Downtown

City Hall

Everyone who has ever seen the 'Superman' television series with the late George Reeves will recognise City Hall as the fictional Daily Planet building. 'Dragnet' also used it in that show's opening credits.

City Hall was opened in 1928 and was the only building to exceed the 150 foot height limit which was in force until 1957 due to the earthquake fear.

The central, stepped tower is surrounded by smaller wings and is as much a personification of Los Angeles as any of the new, modern glass spires that haunt the horizon up-town.

There is an observation deck on the 27th. floor and escorted tours are available (reservations required).

The Garment District

Making an about-turn and heading South/West to the furthest boundary of **Downtown** bordered by the **Santa Monica Freeway** is the Garment District which spreads over a number of undistinguished blocks. There are several major banks quartered in the district while the California Apparel Mart is a large complex for the garment trade only. However private shoppers will have a field day amongst the clothing bargains from the discount shops along Sth. Los Angeles St. from 7th. St. onwards.

While in the area it is worth going down 8th St towards the Produce Market and stopping at 1228 E 8th St, at **Vickman's Restaurant**. This is pure 1930's Americana. As Vickman's serves the workers and growers at the Produce Market, the restaurant opens at 3 a.m. and closes at 3.p.m. The food is good although heavy on the calorific side (those hefty market workers need all the energy they can get!) and prices are reasonable. The walls are decorated with paintings by artists who live in the area and are for sale (the paintings not necessarily the artists!).

There is a similar old-fashioned eatery called the **Original Pantry Cafe** up at Figuero and 9th. which devotees of plentiful and cheap deli food also frequent.

> **INFOTIP:** Architecture enthusiasts will enjoy the varying styles of homes in the city. The knowledgeable can even track the progress of the spreading city with the different types of houses.

Downtown

Upper Downtown

'Cold cash' would be an apt phrase to sum up this part of town. Bounded by **Grand Avenue, Hollywood Freeway, Harbor Freeway** and **7th Street**, this forest of concrete-and-glass peaks reeks of wealth and Big Business but has a coldness typified by the deserted pavements. As a pedestrian wandering through the solitary canyons of steel one longs for another human face be it only a drunk or a panhandler, or, heaven forbid, even another tourist.

The bankers, the lawyers and the corporate heavies who infest the corridors of Los Angeles power here, are really working on an island of privilege surrounded by some of the poorer neighbourhoods of Los Angeles. This island is, in truth, a renaissance for a once elite residential district that fell on bad times. Writing in the 1940's, Raymond Chandler, that superb chronicler of Los Angeles in all its moods, writes of the decaying 19th. century Gothic mansions on **Bunker Hill** inhabited by men 'with faces like lost battles' and women with 'faces like stale beer'. At that time there was even a funicular railway up from Hill Street to the heights of Bunker Hill. Little of that glory is left but a new glory has overtaken Bunker Hill along the west end of 5th. St., and the modern office blocks have created a skyline those men and women with their lost faces could never have dreamed of. Luckily excellent examples of the original architecture can still be seen on the other side of the Hollywood Freeway in the hilly streets of Angelino Heights. And talking of original architecture, several blocks south on Figuero, completely dwarfed by the tall modern towers, is the only early structure to be found in this area, the 8th. Fire Station.

Bonaventure Hotel

If there is one building that captures the ingenious and adventurous spirit of modern L.A. it would have to be the Bonaventure Hotel. Opened in 1978 it features a central, circular, black-glass tower with four similar satellite cylindrical towers. Heading towards its second decade the Bonaventure is still exciting and innovative, making many of the surrounding structures look positively bland. Unfortunately its spectacular, serene exterior is not matched by the immediate interior lobbies which, although certainly spectacular, are as serene as Friday evening at the Los Angeles International Airport. For guests there is a daily lottery in trying to pick the right elevator in the right tower to get to one's room. However, once there, the views from the rooms and especially the lounges and restaurants on

Downtown

the 35th. floor are fantastic and a night-time dinner in this 'eagle's perch' is like sitting above a carpet of sparkling diamonds.

Music Centre

Walking two or three blocks north-east from the Bonaventure Hotel on **North Grand Avenue** brings you to the attractively laid out Music Center complex of three marble buildings housing the performing arts dominated by the **Dorothy Chandler Pavilion**, a massive 3250 seat auditorium which was named for the widow of the publisher of the Los Angeles Times. Until recently it was the venue for the Academy Awards. The Dorothy Chandler Pavilion is the winter home of the Los Angeles Philharmonic (new quarters are under construction nearby) and also hosts the Civic Light Opera Company and the Joffrey Ballet. The **Mark Taper Forum** is a smaller theatre which produces avant garde and pre-Broadway try-outs and is noted for its controversial 1969 opening production of John Whiting's play The Devils which provoked a religious storm and saw Ronald Reagan, then Governor of California, walking out. The third component in the Center is another large auditorium the **Ahmanson Theatre**. The architect of the Music Center was Welton Becket who also designed the famous round Capitol Records Tower in Hollywood. Becket softened the otherwise austere upper level of the Center with pools, sculptures and a computerised fountain.

Bonaventure Hotel

Downtown

Dodger Stadium

Exposition Park

Exposition Park is reached by continuing south along **Figuero** under the **Santa Monica Freeway** and then on for seven blocks. The Park could be said to be dedicated to the proposition of a 'Healthy Mind in a Healthy Body' for the 114-acre park houses not only the grand **Memorial Coliseum**, home of college football, and the Los Angeles Swimming Stadium and Sports Arena but also two superb museums, the California Museum of Science and Industry and the Natural History Museum. Across the road is the campus of the **University of Southern California**. Truly a meeting place of brains and brawn.

Downtown

Angelino Heights

Heading now in the opposite northerly direction along Figuero there is a slight culture shock as suddenly the eye-pleasing, modern office towers vanish as you reach the start of **Sunset Boulevard** and find instead vacant, weed-filled lots, run-down homes, tired little shops and grubby backyard body works. This is the contrary nature of Sunset Boulevard which we will discover as we trace its length from these whimpering beginnings in the back-blocks of Downtown L.A. through the glitz of Hollywood, the palatial parishes of Beverly Hills and Bel Air until it finally tails off with a bang down at the surf beaches of Pacific Palisades.

But, as in any part of Los Angeles, you only have to turn a corner to find a pleasant surprise awaiting. Here you make that turn left several blocks past the intersection of Sunset and Figuero heading west and drive up the steep streets to **Carroll Avenue** and instantly enter a world of wonderful Victorian architecture.

Dating from 1886, Angelino Heights was the first real suburb and was connected with the downtown below by cable car. The 1300 block is listed on the National Register of Historic Places for its superb Victorian wooden homes which have been lovingly restored (to help in this restoration work house tours are organised twice a year - May and Christmas - to raise funds). There are over 50 homes and carriage houses with most in excellent condition. The multi-fronted homes with ornate towers, balconies and doors are a pleasant contrast to the contemporary L.A. skyline below. This has not escaped the film-makers' notice and Carroll Avenue has done service in a range of films being both an Australian 1930's town and a Colorado ski village, which says something for the ingenuity of Hollywood.

Echo Park

Dropping down the western side of Angelino Heights will bring you to this small park which originally provided water for the nearby farms. The layout of the gardens is English and in all occupies only 26 acres. However the semi-tropical plants must have an appeal as the local Samoan community use Echo Park for their annual get-together. Visible from the park is the circular dome of the **Angelus Temple**, based on the Mormon Tabernacle in Salt Lake City. The church is notable for the fiery preachings of the controversial evangelist **Aimee Semple Mcpherson**.

Downtown

Dodger Stadium

On the other side of Angelino Heights, on its very own hill is Dodger Stadium on **Elysian Park Avenue** which can be reached from the **Pasadena Freeway** or from **Sunset Boulevard**. It has been the home of the Los Angeles Dodgers (ex Brooklyn Dodgers) ever since they came across from New York in 1961.

Elysian Park is the second largest park in Los Angeles with 600 acres of parkland, hills and valleys. As well as Dodger Stadium, the **Police Academy** and a fine Arboretum are within the park.

La Plaza, Birthplace of L.A

Hollywood

Covering Sunset and Vine, Mann's Chinese Theatre, Farmers' Market, La Brea Tar Pits, Macarthur Park, Sunset Strip, West Hollywood, Melrose Avenue, Hollywood Bowl.

Shortly after leaving the turn-off to Elysian Park on the right, Sunset Boulevard splits in two. Continuing straight ahead it becomes **Hollywood Boulevard** while the turn to the left, heading west, remains **Sunset** and is the track we will continue to follow. It is here **Sunset Boulevard** starts to take itself seriously. Just prior to the turn off is a faded, run-down cinema called the Vista which like the district appears unloved, although a community campaign to save it from demolition is underway. The sad little picture house a symbol of the Old Hollywood, looks down Sunset towards New Hollywood, personified by the gleaming new studios of the television companies, the offices of the cable networks and the shiny office towers of the financiers and agents.

KCET Studios

As mentioned this early part of Sunset Boulevard as it moves towards its junction with Hollywood Boulevard is of little interest apart from a range of fast food outlets and some interesting, ethnic restaurants.

However at 4401 Sunset, a group of clay-coloured, Spanish style buildings housing the studios of Public Broadcasting TV station, KCET, have some old B-grade movie history enshrined in its bricks and mortar.

These were the studios of **Monogram Pictures** and then later **Allied Artists** when they became a subsidiary of Monogram.

These are the oldest studios in continual use having been first operated in 1912 by the Lubin Manufacturing Company, a film production company from Philadelphia.

KCET conduct weekly tours of their current facilities and also the restored Monogram screening theatre from the 1930's.

Griffith Park

Before we wander off down Sunset Boulevard it would be wise to continue up Hollywood Boulevard to **Vermont Avenue** and turn north to Griffith Park, the largest urban park in the United States.

The 4063 acres were the 1896 gift to the city by wealthy businessman Col Griffith J Griffith who amongst his many achievements, spent a year in San Quentin Prison on an attempted murder charge of his wife.

Hollywood

Griffith Park takes in a region that was once an integral part of the Indian trail system and covers the south-facing slopes of the Hollywood Hills.

Two residential suburbs, **Los Feliz** and **Silverlake**, are part of the Park environs although there is not the studied look of other suburbs as the homes here are built around the contours of the land, not vice versa. One of the more remarkable homes, and something of a Los Angeles landmark, is at 2607 Glendower Avenue. Known as the **Ennis-Brown House**, it was built by Frank Lloyd Wright in Mayan style using concrete blocks. It is certainly a remarkable building and is still a private residence although there are tours on the second Saturday in January, March, May, July, September and November.

One of the most popular features of Griffith Park is the **Observatory and Planetarium**. On clear nights locals come here to observe the stars through the Observatory's telescope or to watch the displays of the stellar system at the Planetarium. James Dean fans will remember the Observatory as the setting for 'Rebel Without Cause'.

Another big hit with Angelenos is the Greek Theatre, which is built amphitheatre style with a Grecian facade. From June through to October the Greek Theatre is the venue for a range of different productions but particularly has a name for the quality rock acts that appear here.

Within Griffith Park there is a wide variety of sporting

Universal Studios

Hollywood

activities with horseback riding and hiking along the trails in the Hollywood Hills being high on the list. There are tennis courts, boating on the Silverlake Reservoir and even two cricket pitches.

Travel Town is both an open air and undercover museum devoted to transport and has a wide selection of old railroad rolling stock, planes, cars, fire trucks and circus wagons.

For those who like zoos, the **Los Angeles Zoo**, opened in 1966, has over 2000 animals in enclosures as close to their natural habitat as possible. There are 75 acres in all.

Most kind of foods are available at restaurants throughout the park's surrounds (even Afghanistan delicacies can be had) and places like La Strada even provide professional singers to serenade the customers whether they like it or not.

Although there have been few problems in recent years with bushfires, in 1933 29 fire-fighters died when caught in flames during a summer blaze.

Hollywood Sign

It's appropriate that one of Hollywood's most famous symbols originally had nothing to do with the movies it has come to represent; like the celluloid images it was manufactured.

The 16.5 metre high sign with its 4000 light bulbs overlooking Tinsel Town on Mount Lee, was originally a real estate sign. It actually read **Hollywoodland** promoting a real estate development which never came about. In the mid-1900's the 'Land' was removed.

Pranksters often make changes to the sign. During the Iran-Contra hearings supporters of the prime witness, Col Oliver North, changed the sign to read '**Ollywood**'.

Before we go back to Sunset Boulevard this is a good point at which to detour through the Hollywood Hills towards the San Fernando Valley and to Universal Studios.

Universal Studios

Back in 1915 moviemaker Carl Laemmle, founder of Universal Pictures, used to charge the public 25 cents to sit on rough planks and watch his crew make silent movies. Afterwards they could buy eggs from 'Uncle Carl's Hatchery'.

The prices have changed, the faces are different, the movies are more sophisticated and there are no eggs for sale, but the principle is still the same. People are fascinated by movies so why not let them pay for the 'privilege' of seeing how they are made.

Hollywood

Having improved on the boss's original concept Universal Studios is now the biggest drawcard in Los Angeles outside Disneyland and attracts over 3 million visitors a year (one in every 15 who come to Los Angeles County).

However don't expect to get a close-up view of a current movie being made. No matter how much the hoping-to-be-a-star, squeaky clean studio guides enthuse about the chance of seeing a 'Star' (everything they say is in capital letters!), the working actors and actresses don't come within a bull's roar of the great unwashed. With a bit of luck you might get a glimpse of some outdoor shooting a kilometre away but the studio is very careful to keep the sets free of distraction.

The public don't complain though for Universal have gone to great lengths to ensure the studio tour is fun.

> **INFOTIP:** Because L.A. is an 'image' town don't be surprised to hear locals talking of the salaries they earn, the type of houses they own and the cars they drive. It is even fashionable to boast about an 'in' pet.

The basis of the tour is a '**Super Tram**' ride through the back lots in a 175 seater set of trams that plough through avalanches, dip through the Parting of the Red Sea, edge past a lagoon where the 'Jaws' shark pops up unexpectedly, crosses a collapsing bridge and braves galactic wars. Of course there is no real danger but it's a lot of fun and well done. For nostalgia buffs the real interest is in the outdoor sets: the fake New York streets, the Mexican village, the Middle European square and the Western town where so much of the studio's product was shot. The streets are lined with the facades of neat Middle America homes, the lovely old Tara mansion from 'Gone With The Wind' and the sinister, Gothic Bates' home from 'Psycho'. A range of props is also on display.

Studios 30 and 32 are reserved for visitors who are given talks and demonstrations of the effects used to create movie illusions.

After the tour the visitors are let loose in the Entertainment Centre where there are live animal shows, stuntmen falling off roofs and various indoor productions such as Castle Dracula where clever sets and costuming can produce the odd chill plus the more up-to-date 'Adventures of Conan'. A Screen Test Theater allows audience participation as extras in a mock-up scene from a previously released Universal picture with the clever editing of the visitors' 'performance' into actual footage.

Hollywood

San Fernando Valley

> **INFOTIP:** Fast food has been raised to an art form in L.A. It is imaginative, cheap and supplied in copious quantities.

There are plenty of fast food outlets and quite good souvenir shops. If looking for something more substantial there are two larger restaurants, **'Womphopper's'** a recreated 1800's style saloon, and **'Victoria Station'** a heavily romanticised version of London's mainline station which will not fool anybody who has seen the dreary reality.

Universal Studios is located at **Universal City** on the **San Fernando Valley** side of the Hollywood Hills looking down over the valley and across to Burbank. It is easily reached along the Hollywood Freeway and is well signposted.

Hollywood

> **INFOTIP:** Although the freeway system looks horrendously jammed and complicated it actually is a good way to travel. Visitors will be surprised at the steady pace of drivers and their good manners.

KTLA Studios

Back on Sunset Boulevard as it turns West after splitting ans spawning Hollywood Boulevard, after several blocks at 5858 is the most elegant building you will see in the Hollywood stretch of Sunset Boulevard. These are the television studios of KTLA housed in a long, white building with a facade of tall columns in the neo-Colonial style. It looks not unlike an 'out-take' from 'Gone With The Wind'. There is something of the elegance of the Nash architecture around Regent's Park in London.

The studios' importance goes back to 1926 when **Warner Brothers** perfected synchronised sound in these studios for their film '**Don Juan**' which preceded by a year their own picture '**The Jazz Singer**' as the first commercial sound film.

In 1929 when Warner's moved to Burbank they still retained the studios for their animated cartoon features and thirteen years later sold the building to Paramount. For a period during the 1940's and 1950s' the world's largest bowling alley was centred here and the studios didn't get back their rightful use until 1962 when **Gene Autry** bought them for his KTLA TV station and KMPC radio station.

Almost next door is a smaller but similarly elegant archway and church. This is the **Church of All Religions**, obviously for those who want to cover their bets!

Gower Gulch

This unprepossessing corner of Gower St. and Sunset was given the name 'Gower Gulch' from its association with the B-grade westerns produced at nearby Monogram Pictures and the other smaller studios located along Gower.

Each day the extras, in cowboy or Indian dress, would gather at the corner hoping to be called for work on that day's shooting. As this was during the 1920's and 1930's when work was scarce it is understandable tempers would get frayed amongst those who missed out on being selected, so unconfirmed reports of actual gunplay between the despondent actors are easy to believe.

On the Eastern side of Gower Street are the Sunset-

Gower Studios which was the first home for **Columbia Pictures** which had been founded in 1920 as the C.B.C./Film Sales Company by brothers Harry and Jack Cohn and Joseph Brandt. with the name being changed to Columbia in 1924. Because of its position on Gower Street which was known then as '**Poverty Row**' because of the number of small, fly-by-night movie companies, and because of the two-reel comedies and short features in which Columbia specialised it earned the soubriquet 'The Corned Beef and Cabbage Company'. Corn is still a product of the studios which are now used for the production of daytime television soaps such as 'Days of Our Lives'.

Cinerama Dome Theatre

In the same vicinity, and on the same side of Sunset in the short block between **Vine** and **Cahuenga**, is the Cinerama Dome Theater, a dinosaur of a picture palace being the last, vast remnant of an intriguing film process which departed with only slightly less speed than most cinematic novelties.

The Cinerama Dome was launched with appropriate Hollywood razzamatazz in 1963 with the film It's a Mad, Mad, Mad, Mad, World.

Cinerama itself was first introduced as Vitarama at the 1939 New York World Fair but its cumbersome eleven-projector system made it impractical for general release. A simplified three-lens method was developed and the process re-launched in 1952 with the travelogue This is Cinerama. It was ten years before the first story feature How The West Was Won was released. But the curiosity value soon wore thin and Cinerama died an unnoticed death.

However, the Cinerama Dome adapted to other film techniques and its excellent sight lines and state-of-the-art equipment assured its future as a movie house but one wonders how long it will be before developers move in with the bulldozers and erect a more 'cost efficient', bland office tower in its place.

The low-rise, geodesic dome at 6360 Sunset looks like a large beehive glinting in the sun and is definitely a Hollywood landmark.

Berwin Entertainment Centre

At 6525 Sunset Boulevard, on the opposite side of the road from the Cinerama Dome and a film-can throw away, is this fine example of Spanish-cum-deco design and a testament to the fact that not every developer want's to rip down the old reminders of Hollywood's past.

Hollywood

Hollywood and Vine at night

The building was formerly the **Hollywood Athletic Club**, where Buster Crabbe was the pool attendant and where John Wayne in his cups would throw billiard balls from the window onto the street below. Most of the major male stars from the 1930's and 1940's would either work out here or stay in the various apartments. Although women were barred the rule was more honoured in the breach.

The first Emmy Awards for television (the name is a corruption of 'Immy' for image orthicon tube) were presented here in 1949.

After a change of ownership, the Hollywood Athletic Club was eventually bought by local businessman Gary Berwin who restored the original decor and turned it into an office centre for record and entertainment companies.

Hollywood and Vine

Since we are in the area, this is a good juncture at which to leave Sunset Boulevard temporarily and head up Vine Street to Hollywood Boulevard to this famous corner which is the start of the 'tourist's Hollywood'.

Hollywood

L.A Civic Centre at night

The corner is renowned more for the image than the actuality, which really sums up Hollywood Boulevard

Hollywood and Vine is just an ordinary intersection with no indication as to why it achieved its notoriety. There are no famous buildings and no stars (the only time a star is seen on Hollywood Boulevard is when he or she inaugurate a personal star on the Walk of Fame).

> **INFOTIP:** Don't let the image of Los Angeles overwhelm you. It is still a city with people going about their everyday jobs.

Pantages Theatre

East of Hollywood and Vine at 6233 Hollywood Boulevard is the exotically florid Pantages Theater. Its impact depends on one's artistic tastes: for many it raises vulgarity to an art form, for others it is classic Hollywood.

Opened in 1929, it was designed by B. Marcus Priteen and named for its owner, Alexander Pantages.

In recent years it has been a venue for stage musicals.

Hollywood

Capitol Records

Just up Vine Street (1750 North Vine) this distinctive building still can turn heads although it is nearly 40 years old.

Designed by the architect **Welton Becket** (he also created the L.A. Music Center) it was supposedly inspired by singer Nat King Cole and writer Johnny Mercer who suggested a building in the shape of a stack or records with a phonograph needle on top. And that's exactly what it looks like.

Just as the round towers of the Bonaventure Hotel represent the sleekness of Downtown Los Angeles so the round Capitol tower symbolises the heartbeat of Hollywood.

The Walk of Fame

For over 3 kilometres of sidewalk the immortals of Hollywood are guaranteed fame, even if it means being walked over and spat on by fellow humans and even worse by dogs.

Nearly 1900 stars from all facets of showbusiness have

Sidewalk Imprints

Hollywood

their names in brass set in a pink star on a square of grey terrazzo paving on both sides of Hollywood Boulevard from Gower to Sycamore and then along Vine from Sunset to Yucca.

The Walk of Fame was inaugurated in 1958 by a group of Hollywood business men as a promotional stunt for Hollywood Boulevard. Eight stars were chosen from the ranks of the ancient and the contemporary: Olive Borden, Ronald Coleman, Louise Fazenda, Preston Foster, Burt Lancaster, Edward Sedgwick, Ernest Torrence and Joanne Woodward.

Then it was an honour, today it is little more than a commercial transaction. Nominees for 'entombment' must have worked in movies, radio, television, records or theatre for at least five years, be approved by the Hollywood Chamber of Commerce and cough up a fee of $3500.

Not every embedded star is real...fictional characters like Snow White also get a place in the Walk of Fame.

Caution needs to be exercised along the pavements as progress is slow and a health hazard due to most pedestrians walking with their heads bowed reading the names. Many a browser has wandered into a lamp-post.

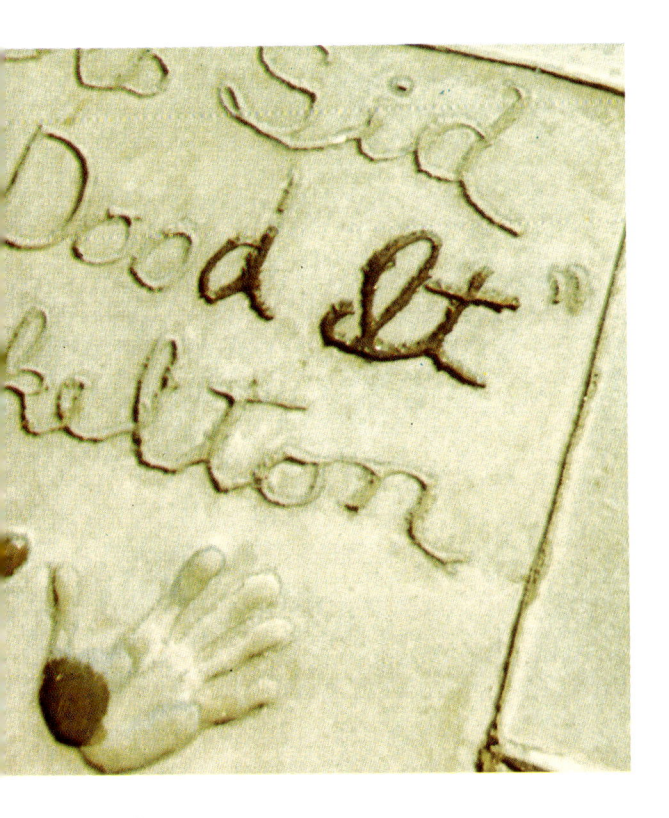

Hollywood

Hollywood Wax Museum

Why anyone would wish to see wax dummies of their favourite stars is a mystery considering most will crop up in first release movies (if young and still alive) or on late-night television (if old and/or dead).

The Museum is at 6767 Hollywood Boulevard.

Mann's Chinese Theatre

When the Mann company brought this famous Hollywood institution, corporate ego demanded the name be changed; however most film aficionados will always remember this by the original name, **Grauman's Chinese Theater**.

At 6925 Hollywood Boulevard, two blocks west of Highland Avenue, the Chinese Theater is the town's most identifiable building after Capitol Records. The facade is 'Over the Top Oriental' and looks like nothing you would ever find in China.

The theatre was built by Sid Grauman in 1927 and was launched with the premiere of Cecil B. De Mille's '**King of Kings**' at which silent movie star Norma Talmadge is supposed to have accidentally stepped in the still-wet concrete. This was capitalised on by Grauman and suddenly Hollywood, a town that loves gimmicks, had a new 'tradition'. After Norma's clumsiness it became fashionable for selected stars to leave their foot-prints, hand-prints, nose-prints (if Jimmy Durante), hoof-prints (if Trigger) and leg-prints (if Betty Grable).

Any morning, afternoon and night, especially when the tourist coaches stop by, the forecourt of the theatre is packed with film fans staring at their favourite star's 'autograph'.

On some days you might get to see a '**living statue**' in action. This is a resting actor who, dressed in black cowboy gear, stands motionless by the side of the forecourt. With special make-up and remarkable breath control he is taken as part of the scenery until there is a sudden movement and the 'statue' springs to life thereby effectively frightening the hell out of anyone standing nearby.

The theatre is still functioning as a movie house with both the original and two newly built cinemas carrying the latest releases.

Almost directly opposite is the **Paramount Theatre** a forlorn reminder of the district's former glory.

Yamashiro

A block past Mann's Chinese Theatre is Sycamore Avenue. Turn right here off Hollywood Boulevard, cross over Franklin and climb the hill to Yamashiro's Restaurant which functions as one of Los Angeles' better Japanese restaurants when not doubling as a movie set.

Yamashiro's with its imported 600 year-old pagoda is set amidst neatly kept miniature gardens and streams and was used as the Officers Club in the Marlon Brando picture **'Sayonara'**.

The view on a hazy day is not particularly attractive for it focuses on the back-yard dross of Hollywood Boulevard but at night the spread of lights hides the daytime ordinariness.

The restaurant was built around 1912 or 1913.

Movieland Wax Museum

The Magic Castle

Coming back down the hill from Yamashiro's practically underneath on Franklin Avenue is The Magic Castle.

You won't be able to go inside unless you are a member or a member's guest but there is no charge for standing and looking at the turn-of-the-century Gothic mansion.

The Magic Castle was built as the home for a banker, served briefly as the domicile of Janet Gaynor and then became a club for magicians and lovers of the dark arts.

Reportedly there is a stuffed owl in the library and to gain

Hollywood

entrance members are required to utter the words '**Open Sesame**' to the impassive bird.

Franklin Avenue ends at Highland Avenue and by following this back into the hills one arrives at the Hollywood Bowl.

Hollywood Bowl

This is a wonderful venue on a summer's evening especially when the resident summer orchestra, the Los Angeles Philharmonic, has scheduled concerts. The Philharmonic has been a fixture at the Bowl since its opening in 1929.

The site of the Bowl was known as Daisy Dell and used to echo to the sound of horses hooves during the silent movie days. Several minor structures preceded the concrete shell which was designed by **Lloyd Wright**, son of the famous father **Frank**.

The natural amphitheatre setting, enhanced by the shell, provides reasonable acoustics although amplification is often required. If sitting in the back rows of the 17,000 seat 'auditorium' you may need powerful binoculars to see the faces of the performers on stage.

It is a Hollywood custom to take a picnic supper to help enjoy the music and the surroundings.

Increasingly the Bowl is used by visiting orchestras and celebrity artists during the summer concert seasons.

Sunset Strip

Once Sunset Boulevard crosses Fairfax heading west, you can sense the change. The wide, former wagon trail which linked **El Pueblo** with the beach, suddenly gets more interesting. It dips and curves and there is a palpable buzz in the air. This is the famed Sunset Strip which runs from Fairfax through to Doheny Drive where Sunset changes character even more dramatically as it enters Beverly Hills.

Nobody can satisfactorily explain how Sunset came to have the tag 'Strip'. A general theory is also mundane: years ago real estate developers sold the land it encompasses as one 'strip'. A more lurid hypothesis ties the name in with the nightclubs and brothels which flourished here.

Anyway, Sunset Strip is the heart of **West Hollywood** which is its own city. Originally called Sherman, its citizens voted against being administered by Los Angeles City and opted for the more general and more lax Los Angeles County. Becoming its own city with an area of only 1.8 square miles (*only slightly larger than the actual City of*

Hollywood

London which is 1 sq. mile) West Hollywood, free of L.A. city restraints, developed into a mini red light district with bars, nightclubs and houses where the ladies were exceedingly friendly. It was a favourite spot for the film elite to unwind after a hard day had streaked their Max Factor.

Today West Hollywood has cleaned up its act. While far from sedate it is infinitely more respectable and the film stars can be seen slipping in through the doors of places like Spago's (where the traditional post-Oscar night party is held) and Nicky Blair's.

West Hollywood is the gay centre of Los Angeles with a range of gay bars and clubs as well as catering for straights who want to be 'daring' with theatre-restaurants such as La Cage Aux Folles which is on **La Cienega** housed in a wondrously pink building which stands out from its drab surroundings like a vegetarian at a butcher's picnic.

West Hollywood is also high on antique shops, interior decorators and design showrooms.

Lovers of celluloid nostalgia are in for a shock. Thanks to the developers, who have no such nostalgic feelings, two of the Strip's most famous landmarks have been razed.

The distinctive portico at 8524 Sunset which became known to millions of TV viewers as the entrance to '77 Sunset Strip' has vanished along with the restaurant it decorated, which was famous in its own right as Dino's Lodge and for its owner Dean Martin.

A greater crime was the demolition of Schwab's Drugstore at 8024 Sunset. Not even the facade has been kept of a place which was the scene of a thousand dreams and one enormous myth. Yes, Virginia, there is a Santa Claus. No, Virginia, Lana Turner, the famous 'Sweater Girl', was not discovered sitting at the soda fountain at Schwab's. It is now accepted this was the concoction of the MGM publicity machine. Funnily enough though, there is no real story of how Lana Turner, described by one critic as having 'sluggish carnality', ever grabbed that first break into showbusiness. At the time the story did wonders for Schwab's with a daily parade of young 'hopefuls', male and female, traipsing in to sip sodas and await fame and fortune. Because of this Schwab's became part of the fantasy fabric that is Hollywood and the demise of the drugstore and the failure to preserve is a form of 'cultural' vandalism.

Chateau Marmont

Hollywood, being what it is, thrives on the weddings, divorces, scandals, affairs and deaths of the famous. It is part of the continuing process of ensuring that we, the

Hollywood

humble general public, realise they are not as other mortals but are god-like creatures who live on some vague Olympian plateau with the other deities of the modern world (newspaper tycoons, ageing society matrons and drug-dealers). In this Elysian world no-one goes to the bathroom, no-one spends hours in supermarket queues, no-one puts out the garbage and no-one dies in their own bed.

Hence every slightest infidelity let alone major scandal is carefully chronicled and regurgitated at regular intervals especially by tour-coach drivers.

That's why the first thing you will be told as you drive past the Chateau Marmont (8221 Sunset just west of Crescent Heights Blvd.) is that comedian and actor John Belushi died within its walls of a drug overdose. In fact it is probably the only thing you will be told about this handsome pile of bricks and mortar which has been home to the celebrities since 1929 when it opened on a Sunset Boulevard which was still an unpaved road.

Otherwise you might just overlook this hotel which, because of its position on the high side of the road, the amount of shrubbery, the discreet signage and the general dullness of immediate surrounds, is not instantly conspicuous.

Built in Normandy-chateau style the Marmont has remained a favourite with name visitors despite the fact it is away from the fashionable areas of Beverly Hills and Bel Air. And while it is interesting to hear of it being home to Boris Karloff and those two notorious recluses Howard Hughes and Greta Garbo it seems re-assuring the hotel has not been ignored by the new generation like Sting, Richard Gere, John Lennon and Dustin Hoffman; and if they happen to suicide it is almost an affirmation that death as well as life is always done in style, Hollywood version.

'Rock Row'

Since rock 'n' roll got its act together in the 1960's it seemed to follow that Sunset Strip would be the natural place to centre all the action. This has happened and the Strip would now be in line for the title as the world's rock capital.

Undoubtedly **The Roxy** at 9009 Sunset is the most famous rock venue. Any rock act of note has played there along with top jazz groups. Like most of the clubs on the Strip it looks a little ordinary from the outside. However, that could not be said about **Gazzarri'S** (9039 Sunset) whose entrance is flanked by a huge mural of Mr. Gazzari looking as though he was dressed by Al Capone, which is part of the gimmick as he bills himself as 'The Godfather

Hollywood

Music Centre Complex

Hollywood

of Rock & Roll'. The most familiar name is **The Whisky a Go Go** (8901 Sunset) however the 'Whisky' is now not such a force to be reckoned with as in the early days of '**Go Go Girls**' and other such ancient delights.

At 8433 Sunset is the top comedy club in town **The Comedy Store** which is one of a rash of comedy outlets where new talent is given a chance. Some are excellent like The Comedy Store or the original, **The Improvisation** (or 'Improv': two branches, one on Melrose and one on Santa Monica) where Robin Williams and Bette Midler got their break. Others are just ordinary bars with a couple of lukewarm and cheap (to the owners) amateur comedians.

Sunset Strip can also offer star-watchers a couple of popular celebrity haunts where the food and service is still good in spite of it. **Spago's** looks out on the Strip but the entrance is in Horn Avenue and **Nicky Blair's** is part of an office block at 8730 Sunset. **Le Dome** is another popular restaurant in its own elegant premises at 8720 Sunset.

In this area you will also find **Sunset Plaza** which is a group of fashionable and up-market specialty shops, boutiques and small cafes where the patrons sit out on the pavement under umbrellas a la European cafe style, except without the style.

Marking the end of Sunset Strip, the interesting part anyway, is **Tower Records** whose original home base at 8801 Sunset has always been a Mecca for record fans of all ages and tastes. On the other side of the road is **Book Soup** noted for a good collection of literary works and foreign publications. Just around the corner at 1020 Nth. San Vincente is **Le Bel Age** a stunningly decorated and serviced hotel hiding behind a very plain facade.

Melrose Avenue

Running east to west from the Hollywood Freeway to Santa Monica Boulevard, Melrose Avenue is fairly quiet during a weekday but comes alive at night and at weekends when the youth fraternity hit the streets in a parade of gear and hairstyles that create new limits of invention. Weird and wonderful they parade and preen to everyone's satisfaction, especially their own.

Melrose is home to a range of interesting boutiques with names like **Mad Man, Koala Blue** (owned by expatriate Australian film and record star Olivia Newton-John), **Wacko Gifts, A Star is Worn** and **Retail Slut**.

Restaurants zero in on the young market with one of the most popular being **Johnny Rocket's Diner** (7507 Melrose), a Fifties-style eatery with decor from that decade and juke boxes blaring early rock-and-roll.

The Melrose area is also home to **Paramount Pictures**,

Hollywood

the only major studio to remain in the Hollywood area.

Paramount has the only recognisable set of gates in the industry. The embossed archway with the four 'barley-sugar' twists of supporting pillars has been used to good effect in scores of movies (Paramount's of course) but are no longer part of the main entrance. They have been preserved at their location on Marathon St. but the official, more pedestrian entrance is on Melrose Avenue.

Jesse Lasky, one of the co-founders of Paramount Pictures, is buried close to his work in a crypt at **Hollywood Memorial Cemetery**, 65 acres of graveyard on Santa Monica Boulevard backing onto the walls of Paramount. It is not as ornate or as vulgar as Forest Lawn but has a nice roster of stars who have found their one last plot. Former jail-bird and 'taxi dancer', Rudolph Valentino is the most noted internee if only for the faithful 'lady in black' who used to leave flowers on his grave on the anniversary of his death (Valentino died in 1926). Apparently age has finally caught up with the devoted fan who is either infirm or sharing the Great Desert in the Sky with 'The Sheik'.

At the western end of Melrose Avenue at Robertson Boulevard near Santa Monica is the **Pacific Design Centre** dubbed 'The Blue Whale' by residents because of its colour and its size. It is magnificently ugly but just seems to suit L.A. The complex is a rabbit warren of superb furniture and interior design shops, which sell only to the trade although a foreign visitor who looks suitably 'cashed up' may get the chance to buy a particular piece he or she fancies (and we don't mean the staff!).

Fairfax District

Stretching from Hollywood Boulevard to the Santa Monica Freeway Fairfax Avenue has the most visible Jewish community area in the Los Angeles County. It is home to synagogues, Jewish community centres, Jewish businesses and so many delicatessens and food stores that a three-block length of Fairfax is affectionately known as 'Kosher Canyon'. The most famous of the deli's is **Canter's** at 419 South Fairfax which is open 24 hours and is noted for its pastrami, noise and unpredictable service.

At the corner of Fairfax and Beverly Boulevard is **CBS/Television City** which was built in 1952 with extensions in 1976. The huge 'Eye' on the facade will readily identify the studios which otherwise have that bland, modern look of television studios around the world. If you wish to look through the best way is with the free audience tickets to the many game shows and soap operas filmed inside.

Around the corner in Beverly Boulevard are two

Hollywood

interesting examples of the kind of architecture that Los Angeles revels in. At 7600 Beverly is the **Pan Pacific Auditorium** the 1938 auditorium built in what has been described as 'Streamline Moderne'; while at 7415 there is a miniature medieval castle with drawbridge and moat which is the **A.J. Heinsbergen Building** named for the design company that erected it in 1925.

But the biggest drawcard on Fairfax, at the corner of Third St, is **Farmer's Market**. Although an interesting slice of Angeleno life, it is hard to fathom just why every coach tour of Hollywood stops here (an estimated 40,000 tourists and locals call in each day). The market opened in 1934 as a co-operative for the local farmers. Nowadays it is less co-operative and more competitive. Still there are wonderful fruit and vegetable stalls as well as a good range of gourmet food shops. The Market also has some of the best souvenir shops on the tourist route especially if you like kitsch and antiques which are in abundance on the Fairfax Avenue side in the Showcase Gallery where various antique dealers lease space in one of the showcases with Gallery staff selling on a commission basis. The range of wonderful objets d'art is excellent particularly if you fancy 1930's and 1940's movie trivia.

Farmers Market

Hollywood

Wilshire Boulevard

Like Sunset Boulevard, Wilshire wanders a rambling journey through Los Angeles from the Downtown area up through Beverly Hills and Westwood before gradually expiring on the beaches of Santa Monica. Despite this rather lengthy trip the most interesting part of Wilshire Boulevard is a relatively short section from just outside the Downtown limits up to Rodeo Drive. And although it has a glitzy look, Wilshire is notable more for its cultural and financial status rather than the normal show-business aura.

Macarthur Park was not just a figment of Richard Harris' musical imagination when he recorded the song of that title with the oddest lyrics this side of 'Tutti Frutti'. It is an actual park which was originally called Westlake Park but was re-named in 1942 in honour of the famous U.S. military commander. The 32 acres of parkland between Alvarado and Park View is a pleasant foreground to the high-rise office towers that border its greenery. Some of the sculptures may be a little unusual but the gardens and the array of trees, shrubs and plants add a peaceful note. Popular in the daytime it is best avoided at night, which applies to most of the parks in L.A. Incidentally some of the side streets in the immediate vicinity, such as **South Bonnie Brae Street** have some excellent examples of Victorian architecture.

Just past the corner of Vermont is the site of the once-famous **Ambassador Hotel** whose **Cocoanut Grove** was the nightclub legend of Hollywood from the 1930's to the 1950's, alas no more. From Marion Davies riding a horse through the lobby to the assassination of Robert Kennedy, the Ambassador had the richest store of Hollywood history and scandal which read like the wildest creation of a studio script-writer. It was the playground of the stars and a regular mother-lode of scuttlebutt which was expertly mined by the two 'Dragons of Gossip', columnists Hedda Hopper and Louella Parsons. By 1968 when Robert Kennedy was shot down in the Ambassador's kitchens the star was starting to wane and the tragedy only hastened its decline into oblivion.

A large slab of the Mid-Wilshire area, bordered by Pico, Western, Vermont and 3rd., has been given the name **Koreatown**. The reason is obvious as practically every flight from Seoul drops off new immigrants looking for the Promised Land. They tend to gravitate towards this section of Los Angeles which, if not exactly the Promised Land, at least gives the South Koreans more of an opportunity away from the crowded competitiveness of their home country.

The new settlers will quickly assimilate as the 'old

Hollywood

Rancho La Brea Tar Pits

hands' have gone to a deal of trouble recreating something of the 'old country' here in the urban wilderness. Shop and store fronts are decorated with Korean lettering and, in many cases, have Korean style architecture. Korean language newspapers, Korean food stores and Korean decorative touches have established a definite presence although this is still a long way from being a tourist attraction (and maybe the local residents should be thankful for that!). Whether this clannishness is good for assimilation in the long run is another matter but at least it adds flavour to the stewpot that is Los Angeles. As an aside, it was interesting to note in one Korean shopping centre there was one store which boldly proclaimed itself the 'Canaan Bakery'.

On Wilshire Boulevard between La Brea and Fairfax is the so-called **Miracle Mile** which developed out of a 1930's shopping and office district and was promoted as the place to spend your cash in Los Angeles. It eventually went into decline but restoration work and careful preservation has kept the Mile as an attraction for those who love art deco. More important is **Hancock Park**, not because it is a park but because it is the site for the **La Brea Tar Pits**. The pits were first formed 35,000 years ago but it wasn't until this century that archaeologists discovered the rich treasure trove of fossilised plants and animals that had become stuck there. The story of the tar pits can be seen in a short documentary film which screens at the nearby **George C Page Museum of La Brea Discoveries** which also has a fine collection of Ice Age fossils. To complete your cultural circuit of Hancock Park there is the **Los Angeles Country Museum of Art** stocked with excellent relics and craftwork from all areas of American culture. The trustees have spread their nets wide to gather in a rich spectrum of Asian and European artefacts including a pleasing selection of Old Masters. There is also a 500-seat auditorium for regular concerts.

The prime eating house in the area is considered to be **Chasen's** at 9039 Beverly Boulevard. The building looks slightly barn-like from the side which is possibly why it appeals to Old Hollywood, especially former cowboys like Ronald Reagan and Jimmy Stewart. It does not take credit cards but if you are a star you can open an account (you need to be a star recognised by Chasen's and not just in your own estimation).

Beverly Hills

Covering Beverly Hills, Bel Air, Century City, Westwood, Brentwood.

Next to Hollywood this is the best known name in the whole of Southern California. In fact it is linked with Hollywood in a complementary way as the plush residential enclave from which the stars emerge each morning, like moles blinking in the daylight, to be whisked off to propound their art in the fantasy studios of Tinsel Town before scuttling back again at night. In truth they are as likely to be filming in New York, on the non-rainy plains of Spain or in the jungles of Thailand as in Hollywood whose studios now basically service the needs of television.

Many of the modern stars have left the oppressive luxury of Beverly Hills for the freedom of country estates. Still there are enough of the old time stars around to make the obligatory tour of the movie homes of Beverly Hills an attractive option for the visitor even if he notices that the tour guides regularly refer to the 'previous', 'former' or 'ex' homes of the stars. Today, Beverly Hills is the preserve of the professional people: lawyers, doctors (particularly heart surgeons), psychiatrists and stock brokers.

The Beverly Hills administration has taken great care to ensure that their residents live in untroubled comfort. They can't do much about the roaring traffic along Santa Monica,

Beverly Hills

Wilshire and Sunset Boulevards which ploughs regardless through the sacrosanct city nor can they ban the lumbering tourist coaches invading the quiet streets, but they do have other measures to keep Beverly Hills unique.

The first is most obvious when travelling along Sunset Boulevard and crossing the dividing line with West Hollywood at Doheny Drive. Immediately you will notice there are no billboards - they are banned in the City of Beverly Hills. Similarly you will find no hospitals, funeral parlours or cemeteries within the city's boundaries, obviously on the assumption that everyone is too rich and famous to sicken let alone die. Nor will you find any gas stations, so chauffeurs have to trundle to a less salubrious neighbourhood to fill up the Maserati, the Cadillac of the drop-head Rolls Royce coupe. Apartment buildings are also out but there are no objections to hotels. The **Beverly Hills Post Office** is the only post office in the world to offer valet parking and there are reports that the Beverly Hills High School has its own oil well! In other words, Beverly Hills does consider itself a tasteful oasis in a desert of flashy vulgarity. So possibly it is not wise to remind the residents that the area was once noted for its lima beans and not its canned celebrities.

> **INFOTIP:** In the upmarket end of town, around Beverly Hills, Westwood and Bel Air, don't expect to see many residents walking. Everybody uses a car. This gives the streets an eerie feeling and makes the walking visitor quite conspicuous.

The first sign of life was a 4500 acre ranch which established in 1810 by a soldier's widow, **Maria Rita Valdez**. When Wilbur Cook designed the initial layout of Beverly Hills in 1907 it was to have been called **Morocco** but eventually this was dropped in favour of the present name inspired by another developer, **Burton E. Green**, who called it after his farm in Massachusetts. The first notable building was the **Beverly Hills Hotel** which was constructed in 1912 and has been pre-eminent ever since with its famed Polo Lounge as the place to be seen and to see which makes it a bit like the cattle market it was in its early ranch days. Since the hotel was sold to one of the world's richest men, the **Sultan of Brunei**, it has been rumoured the hotel will be converted into a private residence which has shaken the Martini Set down to its frilly knickers.

The seal was set on Beverly Hills as a desirable district in which to put down roots when the romantic darlings of America, Douglas Fairbanks and Mary Pickford built **Pickfair** (1143 Summit Drive) in 1912.

Beverly Hills

Movie Stars Homes

Homes are still the prime fascination in Beverly Hills both with those who own them, those who hope to own them and those, like you and me, who will never ever get the faintest chance to own them but just love to 'stickybeak'.

Kerbside vendors near Doheny Drive sell maps to the star's homes for those who wish to wander at leisure rather than rely on the normal, hurried coach tour on which, the driver/guide will inevetably boast of the number of loveable stars who will wave to him as an old friend as he manoeuvres his great bus along the gracious streets. Its amazing just how many stars these driver/guides see putting out the garbage or wandering the front lawn in their night clothes. Even more amazing, the coach passenger never sees any of these things.

> **INFOTIP:** If you must take one of these tours choose a company which offers the small buses as they can get into the higher reaches of Beverly Hills where the normal bus go!.

Beverly Hills

Candlelight Concert

The entrance most used to tour Beverly Hills is Whittier Drive off Sunset Boulevard near the Beverly Hills Hotel but really you can start anywhere off Sunset just as long as you head North, as just no celebrity, movie or otherwise, lives South of Sunset unless an eccentric. It is said that when Beverly Hills was being developed it was deliberately designed to have two 'sides of the tracks' with the wealthy keeping to this exclusive district while the hired help had to fend for themselves on the Westside along Olympic Boulevard.

The avenues of Beverly Hills are most pleasant places to wander not only for the surroundings but for the peace and quiet. Strangely enough this can be initially un-nerving when you realise there is no-one outside enjoying it all. You never see kids kicking a football in the street nor spot a family having a barbecue in the backyard. There are only the Hispanic gardeners tending flower beds. Then you notice the barred windows on most of the homes and the security signs on the front lawn promising 'Armed Response' and you get this eerie feeling that the good burghers of Beverly Hills spend their time in their fortified homes hiding and waiting for some thug to break in. One can almost sense the paranoia.

Beverly Hills

Rodeo Drive

A favourite star-spotting street except the stars will generally avoid it like last year's flop movie especially at weekends when Rodeo is packed solid with gawking visitors and 'pretenders'. Those celebrities who can afford to shop here do so on weekdays, discreetly slipping into Courreges, Hermes, Bijan (appointments only, definitely no walk-in trade), Celine or Chanel when few sightseers are around. The flash cars, whose occupants all look so super-cool in their designer jeans and 'shades', generally belong to used-car salesman who have exceeded their monthly quota. Saturday and Sunday afternoons are the most popular times with visitors who certainly are single-minded about Rodeo Drive. They will jostle and bustle along the pavements as though it were Disneyland and yet one only has to turn a corner to be instantly alone.

Rodeo Drive runs down from Santa Monica Boulevard west towards Wilshire where it meets the **Beverly Wilshire Hotel** with its subdued 1928 baroque facade being matched by the more recent 1971 addition behind the hotel. It is one of a clutch of fashionable hotels in Beverly Hills and while it may not have the showbiz

Beverly Hills

panache of the Beverly Hills Hotel it has a cachet amongst the conservative wealth which gives it a special aura. From here Rodeo continues on to Olympic Boulevard but by now has lost its magic appeal and is a run-of-the-mill residential street.

Along Santa Monica Boulevard from the intersection with Wilshire, is one of the many fancy country clubs that dot this upper part of town. This club prides itself on the fact that it bars show-business personalities. Ronald Reagan was allowed in only when he became Governor of California.

Back up on Sunset Boulevard approaching **UCLA** are two massive wrought iron gates guarding an avenue that enters through a grove of high trees into the swishest part of all Los Angeles County.

Bel Air

This is the home of Old Money and some brash New Money. The curving, hilly roads wind amidst some of the loveliest properties you will ever see. The sense of wealth is over-powering. Of course many of the mansions cannot be seen, being shielded by high walls and thick shrubbery. One can only drive past in awe at the spread of such estates as that which belonged to the late Conrad Hilton.

Memorial Coliseum

Beverly Hills

At times you do get a glimpse into this rarified world such as the house whose large pool is well above the roadway and is liberally dotted with portholes so the hoi polloi can stand outside and glimpse their betters cavorting under water. Pools, of course, are de rigueur in Bel Air and they come in all shapes and sizes. The most unusual looking pool, but practical all the same, belonged to the late Olympic swimming star and film Tarzan, Johnny Weismuller. It runs like a deep narrow canyon the length of his former property enabling the star to do continuous if somewhat claustrophobic laps.

The most remarkable house is within several blocks of Sunset and belongs to the mega-millionaire, television producer Aaron Spelling and it is ostentatious even by Hollywood standards.

However, there is one star who doesn't take himself too seriously and that's Robert Wagner, whose home on Sunset Boulevard near Westwood has a series of quirky statues on the roadside lawns. These are not your normal fake Greek Gods much loved among those who think they are cultured but are actual sculptures of a group of tourists taking photos of the house.

> **INFOTIP:** If walking through Bel Air take care as there no footpaths and the narrow roads run practically to the fence lines. While it may be fun to be run over by your favourite star insurance companies are less impressed.

Century City

If, as the developers intended, Century City is a glimpse of the future then the future looks bleak. The kindest and most universally accepted description is 'sterile'.

Century City's name was derived from **Twentieth-Century Fox** whose studios occupy the Pico Boulevard frontage. Originally the land was the studio back lot extending north to Santa Monica Boulevard. In the 1950's, the studio, facing huge costs incurred with its block-buster extravaganza, 'Cleopatra', decided to sell off this valuable chunk of land. The developers and the architects moved in and before you could say 'Planet of the Apes' a vision of the 21st Century had arisen on the vast acres.

The **Avenue of the Stars** runs grandly down the centre from Pico Boulevard to Santa Monica Boulevard where the main feature of Century City is to be found - the complex of tall insurance buildings and the distinctive, twin angular **Century Plaza Towers**. They are worth seeing at sunset when they become two high slabs of gold. It is interesting

Beverly Hills

to note the architect was Minoru Yamasaki who also designed the original main building for the **Century Plaza Hotel**, directly opposite. The styles are so different with the sharp modern features of the Towers contrasting with the distinctly sixtyish feel of the semi-circular Hotel. The Century Plaza Hotel has since added a Tower Block which was inaugurated by former President Ronald Reagan who always used the hotel as his Californian base while in the White House. The Tower and the underground passage which links it with the main building are decorated with so many sculptures and works of art the hotel issues a catalogue of descriptions.

As part of the Century Plaza Towers are the **Shubert Theatre** and the **ABC Entertainment Centre** which contain a large, legitimate theatre hosting Broadway musicals plus a range of cinemas. Restaurants and deli's are to be found along the lower levels.

The Century City Shopping Center fronting directly onto Santa Monica Boulevard has further cinemas, two major department stores, Bullock's and Broadway, and a variety of boutiques and specialty shops. An imitation 'old-fashioned' market building, complete with sawdust on the floor houses a number of fast food outlets with a wide range of cuisines from a branch of the New York Deli to Japanese and Chinese 'take-outs'.

A block or so to the east along Olympic Boulevard is the black-glassed Century City Medical Centre which has an oil well in its rear yard. And that could only happen in L.A.

The Twentieth-Century Fox studios, at the corner of The Avenue of the Stars and Pico Boulevard, are not open to tours although special requests of a V.I.P. nature can be considered. Still visible through the gates are the remains of the famed New York street set, complete with overhead rail lines, used in the musical 'Hello Dolly'.

Unfortunately Century City for its all deification of things modern is a curiously bleak place for the pedestrian. The awesome contemporary buildings used as backdrops for movies set in the next century have a de-humanising effect and to wander the plazas and the surrounds is to feel alone. Even at peak times when the thousands of office workers who toil unseen in the tall towers finish for the day, they move silently and quickly like characters from some Orwellian novel. It is rather depressing.

Westwood Village

The name is something of a misnomer for Westwood hardly conforms to the European idea of a 'village'. Still, it does have a pleasant, communal atmosphere that belies the fact it is the shopping centre for the neighbouring

Beverly Hills

U.C.L.A. campus and its 30,000 students.

Westwood in fact owes its beginning, as well as its current livelihood, to the university. As late as the early 1920's the district was one vast ranch which had been in existence for eighty years. At the **Westwood Playhouse** is a display of photos which show the districts remarkable growth in seventy years.

If one looks at adjacent Beverly Hills and Bel Air it is apparent that the evolution of Westwood would have occurred anyway, but the establishment of U.C.L.A. in 1929 was the incentive the developers needed to promote the gentle hills of the sprawling ranch as a desirable residential area.

With the exception of the playing fields and campus grounds of the University those wide open spaces have been quickly swallowed up. In their place has risen a self-contained city of high-rise apartment buildings that swamp that swamps Wilshire Boulevard, the still cosy but trendy avenues of Westwood Village, the neat, suburban homes along the side streets and the ordinary, down-market spill around Santa Monica Boulevard.

U.C.L.A. is best seen during vacation time when a sense of calm descends over the campus, although many students remain in residence.

Capitol Record Building

Beverly Hills

The drive around the campus is a nice break from the unnerving streams of traffic along bordering Sunset Boulevard. The landscaping has been done with care and the mixture of pines, firs and eucalypts add a delightful aromatic touch on a warm day.

Most of the buildings have that bland, forgettable look of educational institutions the world over, although one or two, including **Royce Hall**, are built in mock period style. Royce Hall is the venue for frequent recitals and concerts so it is worth checking local newspapers or the University for dates and performers.

Just off campus are the various fraternity houses providing meeting facilities and accommodation for the select few who become members. Land values and the pleasing nature of most of the large homes which provide these residences, the students are obviously not short of dollars.

The heart of Westwood Village is the three blocks between Gayley Avenue and Glendon Avenue. It is a comfortable, low-key mixture of shops primarily aimed at the campus market. Record and book stores seem to dominate as well as restaurants and coffee shops. Names like The Good Earth, Alice's Restaurant, Yesterday's, Tower Records and T.J. Cinnamon say it all. Olivia Newton-John has opened a second branch of her Koala Blue store on Westwood Boulevard although the emphasis is more L.A. than Down Under.

Pride of the Village is the **Village Theatre**, formerly the Fox Theatre whose name still adorns the great Spanish tower which has been a Westwood landmark since the cinema opened in 1931. Across the road on the opposite corner is the less intrusive but still good-looking Bruin Theatre, another of the several film houses which gained for the Village a name as the prime try-out spot for new movies.

Lovers of live theatre flock to the Westwood Playhouse which grew out of furniture showrooms. The owners had originally built the venue to sell their range of imported Scandinavian furniture but as the husband has been a trained singer a natural theatrical interest resulted in the addition of an intimate 498-seat theatre where the owners like to boast, Nick Nolte got his first break. The furniture showroom is still there in the 'foyer', and as well there is a courtyard restaurant, with the whole complex hidden behind high walls, vines and trees.

The 'Village' is also noted for two 'monuments', one to the living and one to the dead. The former is the thoroughly delectable **Westwood Marquis Hotel** whose tall, plain concrete tower (thankfully softened by tall trees and creepers) hides an elegant interior where under-stated luxury is the keynote. It is worth calling in for a drink in the lounge or for the very proper English afternoon tea. The other 'monument' is the **Westwood Memorial Park** which is at 1218 Glendon Avenue. This is the cemetery where Marilyn Monroe and Natalie Wood are buried with both graves (or rather 'crypts') being focal points for fans.

Brentwood is a buffer zone between the plushness of Beverly Hills and Westwood and the down-market breeziness and gusto of Santa Monica and Venice. Brentwood has retained a country town feel and to drive around some of the side streets is to see a homelier side to the Westside of L.A. The bigger homes lie along San Vincente Boulevard, sedately hidden behind tall hedges and miniature forests. San Vincente is famous for the rows of Coral Trees which line the central dividing strip. Brentwood Village carefully cultivates a rustic image helped by the old post office, one of the oldest in the country.

Beaches

Covering Malibu, Pacific Palisades, Santa Monica, Venice, Marina del Rey.

Santa Monica

Some say all roads lead to Rome. Well, in Los Angeles the main ones lead to Santa Monica where Wilshire, Sunset and Santa Monica Boulevards all collapse exhausted on the wide sands fronting the Pacific Ocean. In all truth the sands are the loveliest part for most of actual Santa Monica is uninspiring, to say the least.

A sentimental legend says it was named by Father Juan Crespi who was inspired by the tears shed by Saint Monica for her son who later gave up a dissolute life to become Saint Augustine.

Santa Monica manages to embrace a wide variety of lifestyles. The city is most catholic in its tastes (pun intended!). There are the rich and famous, the rich but not famous, the up-and-coming apprentice Yuppies, the retirees, the drifters and the Average Joes.

Best place to start is at the corner of Ocean Avenue and Santa Monica Boulevard in the shadow of City Hall whose tower tries to ape the more impressive one in Downtown L.A. From the beach side of Ocean Avenue you can get a bus for the trip to Venice Beach but a leisurely 30 to 40 minute walk along the beach-front is more interesting.

Almost immediately below, stretching out into the ocean like a wrinkled old finger, is the famous **Santa**

Beaches

California Beaches

Monica Pier which has seen duty in 'Funny Girl', 'The Sting' and 'They Shoot Horses Don't They?' The Pier is listed on the National Register of Historic Places and is worth a visit for the Carousel which is now into its seventh decade. The quick food stalls and the concrete paths and walls at the entrance to the Pier are a touch depressing but like most seaside piers there is a certain nostalgic charm.

Walking South, it is easier to take the footpath rather than the beach don't mistake the bicycle and skateboard path for the pedestrian track or you'll be busier than a toad on a griddle avoiding the speedsters.

At weekends you will see the park benches near the Pier filled with intent chess players. However, by the time you get to **Venice Beach** the cerebral will have been replaced by the physical. On a Sunday afternoon the strip along Venice known as Ocean Walk is packed tighter than the jeans on the participants in this weekly orgy of egoism. Every male is intent on bursting veins with muscles like cart-horses while every female looks as though she is auditioning for a Playboy centre-fold. Frankly, it's a voyeur's delight. Those who don't have the necessary attributes will try to rate attention in other ways: rap-dancing to ghetto-

Beaches

Coastal View

blasters, juggling knives on unicycles, doing remarkable acrobatics on skateboards or just simply dressing their dogs up in hats and dark glasses. The foreshore becomes one big talent show. To be honest, some of it ain't half bad either!

The big draw card is **Muscle Beach**. As the budding Stallones strut their stuff on the sand the serious business gets under way on a strip of asphalt surrounded by a wire fence. Here an outdoor gymnasium is set up with weights and pulleys and a regular group of participants gather to work out for the watching crowd. The gravity with which the muscle-bound sweat and strain is quite funny to watch which is why it is such a big attraction.

Surrounding everything is a layer of noise from loudspeakers and spruikers who man the lines of stalls selling T-shirts, sun glasses, Chilli Dogs, rock records and the whole range of usual seaside junk.

The houses and buildings show the effect of the seaspray and the wind and there is an unloved and dejected air about Venice Beach when the crowds drift off.

On some of the side streets running back East towards Venice proper, you can glimpse some of the old charm of

Beaches

the original plan by turn-of-the-century tycoon, Abbot Kinney, to create a piece of the Italian Venice here in Southern California.

Kinney was a remarkable man - certainly by today's standards of single-minded 'tycoonery' - for his interests extended far beyond the realm of making money. Having made his money out of cigarettes, Kinney travelled widely in Asia and Africa. He wrote books as diverse as The Australian Ballot and The Conquest of Death, helped develop the Yosemite National Park, edited a local agricultural journal and practised what he described as 'creative reproduction' by fathering nine children.

So his plans for Venice were evidence of a cultured mind and not just some architectural whimsy.

By the time of the official opening of Venice in 1905 his architects and engineers had created a 'folly' on a grand scale: canals had been created, arched bridges built and colonnaded plazas had appeared in the quiet coastal village. Kinney imported gondolas and singing gondoliers and also a flock of pigeons.

Regrettably the local residents failed to understand the concept and after the initial interest and the novelty had waned so did Venice. Most of the canals were filled in during the 1920's as they had become health hazards, the pier Kinney had built decayed and was pulled down and the area generally deteriorated until it was little more than a slum.

However, Los Angeles can point to Venice as an example of the rebirth of a formerly depressed urban district.

The last decade has seen the 'discovery' of Venice as the salubrious place it was those eighty years ago. Artists and writers had long kept the flame flickering but it was the 'new money' of the Yuppie fringe which has set it alight again. Modern developments have sprung up along the ocean front while many of the older areas are getting a new lease of life. Mind you, Venice is a long way from being Beverly Hills but it has a spirit and a sense of 'life' that augurs well for the years ahead.

There is still a long way to go and much of the district is tacky with the 'hinterland' wandering off into some of the poorest sections of L.A. County but, at least, you can claim to see people here and not just empty sidewalks.

If you keep heading South you will find **Marina Del Rey**, the world's largest man-made, boat harbour and stocked with enough examples of maritime wealth to dazzle every boat lover.

From here you can watch the jets thunder in from the ocean to land at **Los Angeles International Airport** referred to by all Angelenos by its airline code, **LAX**.

Marina Del Rey

Pacific Palisades

Turning North from Santa Monica the Pacific Coast Highway passes through Pacific Palisades, from the Spanish palizada or 'stockade, embankment'. This is a reference to the high cliffs both on the beach-front and also back into Topanga Canyon Boulevard and Sunset Boulevard which ends its long journey from Downtown L.A. here, appropriately enough a few metres from the Self Realisation Centre, a free private park for rest and meditation.

Palisades Park off Ocean Avenue is a favourite spot for those who like a great ocean view and has also provided

Beaches

such comfortable living that the area has the highest median level of income within the county, which is ironic considering the Palisades was originally a Methodist communal project.

Pacific Palisades is also the home of an exceptional art foundation, the **J. Paul Getty Museum**.

In some ways the creation of this extraordinary museum mirrors the story of Venice. Like Abbot Kinney, J. Paul Getty was not only a man of enormous wealth but also a man of deep cultural interests with a particular passion for classical history. Also Getty published a book, a fictional work set in the second century B.C. titled 'A Journey from Corinth'.

His fortune enabled Getty to travel the world buying rare Roman and Greek treasures which he housed in a museum built in his ranch home above the beach at Malibu. From there it was a natural and logical step to construct a more elaborate and more suitable home for the Getty collection. Flying in the face of contemporary architectural critics Getty reverted to the past of his dreams and had created a stunning building based on the Roman Villa dei Papiri at Herculaneum at the foot of Mt. Vesuvius whose A.D. 70 eruption destroyed the villa.

The Museum you visit today is the result and was opened in 1974.

A warning: one does need to let the imagination run free otherwise it is too easy to look on the Museum as an architectural freak, along the lines of Disneyland. But on a warm summer's day with the bees humming drowsily amidst the flowers and shrubs and with the cool columns and galleries around the Inner Peristyle and Main Peristyle gardens it takes only the slightest flight of fancy to transport one's mind to the glories of Ancient Rome.

Inside the museum is a trove of fine sculptures and masterly paintings whose restoration work has produced 'as new' works. The collection covers a wide spectrum of art from the days of early Rome through to medieval and modern European masters. Degas, Monet and Cezanne rub artistic shoulders with Carpaccio, Rembrandt, early illuminated scrolls and fourth century busts.

In summer it is not unusual to find a chamber quartet from the Los Angeles Philarmonic giving recitals in the gardens.

The only fly in the ointment are the admission rules. Due to problems with parking in the nearby residential streets admission is only granted to motorists who have booked parking space at the Museum (which needs to be done several weeks ahead), have a parking stub to show that one has used an authorised car park nearby or have a pass given by the bus driver on the buses that use the route along the Pacific Coast Highway. In other words if you are just a pedestrian passing by you cannot go in even though there is no entrance fee. These rules prevent drivers leaving their cars in the residential streets and upsetting the locals.

There are no problems with cars at the **Will Rogers State Historic Park** which fringes Pacific Palisades along Sunset Boulevard. The Park is the former home of the folksy, home-spun, cowboy-cum-philosopher Will Rogers who was America's favourite humourist and whose photos remind one of filmdom's Pa Kettle (actor Percy Kilbride). The Park is a spread of 187 acres and contains Rogers' ranch house, now a museum, plus large playing fields where the stars used to play polo with the tradition still being kept alive with weekend polo games.

Malibu

This 40 km. stretch of prime real estate along the ocean north of Santa Monica is a real imagination-stirrer. The name has a nostalgic ring recalling immediate visions of 50's and 60's movies of the 'Beach Blanket' variety and slick, glossy Doris Day comedies.

In reality, Malibu is less open that one would think. With some of the biggest stars vying for an address in Malibu, and paying through their cocaine-encrusted noses for it, the district has turned in on itself and has become, basically, an exclusive reserve for the wealthy and the notorious. Enclaves like the Malibu Beach Colony are sheltered behind security gates and private beaches protected thoughtfully by a barrier reef. Still, the undeterred film groupie will likely spot a star if prepared to hang out at any of the ritzy shopping malls along the Pacific Coast Highway.

Back into the hills on Las Virgenes Road is the **Malibu Creek State Park**. The Park was once a country club but a large chunk was bought by Twentieth Century Fox in 1946 after finding the site provided useful sets for its pictures. It was then re-named Century Ranch. Fox made extra money out of the ranch by leasing its facilities to other film companies. A variety of films has been shot in part here including the Planet of the Apes series, Love Me Tender, Towering Inferno, the Tarzan movies and How Green Was My Valley for which a whole Welsh mining community was constructed. In recent times Century Ranch has been the site for the top-rating **M*A*S*H** television series and the sets have become a part of the Park's attractions. You can reach the Park along the Malibu Canyon Road but you will find that many of the movie exhibits are a kilometre or so from the main car park so wear 'sensible' shoes.

Outskirts

Nearby Districts

Covering Pasadena, San Fernando Valley, Orange County, Disneyland, Long Beach, Capistrano.

Orange County

If Los Angeles County can be considered as the monument to the total American Dream of prosperity, physical perfection and power, then Orange County, the home of uncomplicated entertainment, is a monument to three individual success stories from that Dream, even if somewhat lacking on the physical perfection side. One of those high achievers was a cartoonist, another a farmer and the third a preacher man. In Orange County stands solid evidence that the trio 'had made it' although it seems crass to point out it is also evidence that 'you can't take it with you'.

The three men were Walt Disney, Walter Knott and Robert Schuller, respectively immortalised in Disneyland, Knott's Berry Farm and the Crystal Cathedral.

Disneyland

Is the jewel of Anaheim, which wouldn't be hard as it is otherwise a featureless city of never-ending, blue collar housing tracts through which freeways rocket as though in a rush to get through.

Walt Disney, whose corpse is kept in a cryogenic state in some Californian icebox conceived Disneyland as a natural offshoot from his movie and marketing empire. It opened in 1955, was an instant hit and has remained so ever since.

The secret of the success is simple. Disneyland allows adults to enjoy a second childhood without fear of ridicule. At the end of the day the biggest smiles are on the parents' faces.

Disneyland is based around four theme zones: Frontierland, Adventureland, Tomorrowland and Fantasyland. In addition there are other attractions such as Main Street which has been carefully constructed to re-create the feel of turn-of-the-century mid-West America, where the nostalgia is so overpowering it makes one wonder whether the 'good old days' were really like this. Still it is a hardened cynic who can enter the gates of Disneyland in the morning and emerge in the evening with the same sceptical attitude. Disneyland has a way of winning over the stoniest heart.

Outskirts

Although not trying to be determinedly trendy, the Disney corporation updates rides and attractions but only after research and meticulous preparation, this also applies to overall upkeep. No matter how many times you visit the Park it is always spotless and immaculate, you'll never see flaking paint, unswept avenues or down-at-heel costumes. The cheerful cleanliness and the clean cheerfulness are overpowering.

For tourists the easiest way to enjoy the fun is with one of the all-day coach tours which pick up at major L.A. hotels in the morning and return from Disneyland around 5.30 pm. There is also a later departure in the evening. The all-inclusive ticket covers the coach transfers and unlimited rides. By car Disneyland is best reached along the Santa Ana Freeway turning off at Harbor Boulevard which is well sign-posted.

More and more tourists stay at Anaheim with excellent accommodation being available including the high-rise, luxurious Hilton, the mock-Tudor Sheraton and the Disneyland Hotel which is linked by monorail with Disneyland itself.

Main Street U.S.A

Outskirts

Knott's Berry Farm

Knott's Berry Farm

Is the other major theme park in the Los Angeles Valley, next door to Anaheim at Buena Park.

The Farm is different from Disneyland not only because it is a theme park devoted basically to one Western theme, but also in its development. Knott's Berry Farm emerged and evolved from another enterprise on the same site whereas Disneyland was a specifically planned development with the location being deliberately selected.

The clue to the origins of Knott's Berry Farm is in the name. In 1920 a venerable T-model Ford chugged along the dirt roads of Orange County bearing Walter Knott and spouse Cordelia who had leased a 20 acre spread 40 kms. southeast of Downtown Los Angeles. There **Walter** planted the newly developed Youngberries while **Cordelia** started cooking chicken dinners which she sold at a roadside stall. The berries were successful but the chicken

Outskirts

dinners were a bigger success and attracted such queues that the Knott's decided to build a small 'ghost town' to amuse those waiting. From there on it was a slow but sure progress to the major amusement complex that today occupies 150 acres. The Knotts also propagated the **Boysenberry**, the hybrid of the loganberry, blackberry and raspberry and named after its 'inventor,' Rudolph Boysen. Knott's Berry Farm has a more casual approach to entertainment without the high technology of Disneyland but this is balanced by the more exciting rides such as the devilish Corkscrew and the Parachute Jump. Similarly, the Farm is best approached along the Santa Ana Freeway taking the off ramps to Valley View Avenue or the later Beach Boulevard. There are also all-inclusive coach tours from L.A.

Crystal Cathedral

At Garden Grove is the type of church one would expect in Los Angeles but it is still impressive. In the shape of a four-pointed star and made of white steel girders and 10,000 panes of glass it soars 40 metres towards its creator's Creator. The church is the brainchild of television preacher Dr. Robert Schuller whose Sunday morning telecasts from the Crystal Cathedral will give you an idea of its magnificence if you can't visit it personally.

The Orange County shore-line provides some interesting day trips especially if you happen to be staying in the Anaheim area.

Anahcim

The main attraction is **Long Beach** where the **Queen Mary** is moored. 50,000 ton, former pride of the Cunard Line, is now a luxury hotel and restaurant complex and offers visitors the chance to experience the wonderful world of old-fashioned shipboard life without getting seasick.

A single ticket will get you onto the Queen Mary and also to the next pier where the **Spruce Goose**, the world's largest wooden airplane which had just one flight in 1947 for its eccentric inventor, Howard Hughes.

Laguna and Newport Beach

It is a pleasant drive along the Pacific Coast Highway through **Newport Beach** and then to **Laguna Beach**. Both resorts are pleasant and undemanding and offer good beaches and comfortably modern facilities. Laguna Beach is where John Steinbeck wrote Tortilla Flat although the

Outskirts

town could not have made much of an impression as there is no reference to it in his collection of letters.

Back inland from Laguna Beach is **Capistrano** where the swallows return on every St. Joseph's Day, March 19th. The mission church of **San Juan Capistrano** is one of the oldest buildings in Southern California, the adobe building dating from 1776 when it was founded by **Father Junipero Serra**. The old gardens and the cool cloisters around the church buildings are popular with the hundreds of daily visitors. Walking down the hill, and as long as the tourist coaches don't get you, will bring you to the **Capistrano Depot** where local entrepreneurs have turned the old railroad station into an attractive complex of eateries. You can still catch the Amtrak train from here to Union Station in Downtown Los Angeles.

If you like to see how the suburbanites live, a drive up into the hills between Capistrano and Laguna Beach will give you sweeping views across the ocean and a chance to study the local architecture much of which runs to Californian redwood shingles.

Further inland between Laguna and Anaheim is **Temecula** the launching pad for hot air balloon flights. The sensation is terrific and the views across the orange groves and vineyards to the mountains in the background makes the floating sensation even more pleasurable. After the flight it is customary to wander off to Callaway's Winery for a wine tasting and barbecue lunch.

San Fernando Valley

'The Valley' as it is commonly referred to, is 177 sq. miles of flatland on the northern side of the Santa Monica Mountains. Being surrounded by mountains and with no access to the ocean breezes the Valley is always considerably warmer than the southern Hollywood side. Pollution, trapped in the saucer-like basin, is also heavier.

The San Fernando Valley was once the site for one of the series of Franciscan missions set up throughout California. The prime activity was ranching. The arrival of the Southern Pacific Railroad in 1874, extended from Los Angeles and followed by the Pacific Electric Railway's local tram lines in 1904, attracted the 'townies' and saw the establishment of the major cities of Burbank (named for the doctor and sheep farmer, David Burbank) and Glendale (after a painting fancied by one of the early settlers).

For tourists the main interest is in the number of film and television studios who moved their lots here: Universal, Burbank, NBC and Disney.

Burbank Studios is the home for both Warner Brothers and Columbia Pictures. There are no public tours of the

Outskirts

studios however small VIP tours can be arranged. You will have more luck at NBC, home of Johnny Carson's Tonight Show. The television studios have regular tours as well as offering tickets to tapings of its live and pre-taped productions. NBC is at 3000 W. Alameda Ave. There is also the **Paramount Ranch** at 2613 Cornell Rd. Agoura, off the Ventura Freeway, where you can wander through some of the old Western sets from Paramount's heyday. Each year, in April and May, there is an olde worlde Renaissance Faire where, through the wonders of studio sets you can imagine you are back in 16th century England. However the noise of the overhead jets and the smog does shatter the illusion somewhat.

Glendale's most notable contribution to the motion picture arts is **Forest Lawn** where the mighty of Hollywood face the last clapper board and moulder away amidst lush, landscaped gardens, reproduction English village churches and a collection of statuary and paintings that make Disneyland look positively conservative.

Pasadena

Nestling in the foothills of the San Gabriel Mountains, Pasadena (an Indian name meaning '**Crown of the Valley**') is a prosperous, sedate city which likes to let its hair down once or twice a year.

Pasadena has long had a touch of conservatism about it, inherited from the 'Old Money' from the East who had journeyed here to establish winter homes. With their conservative thinking they also brought cultural values which successive generations have inherited as evidenced by the Pasadena Symphony Orchestra, the Pasadena Playhouse and the Norton Simon Museum.

Pasadena also loves football and the rituals that go with it. The Rose Bowl is world famous as is the annual Tournament of the Roses Parade held each New year's Day as a preamble to the Rose Bowl collegiate game. The origins of the Parade are appropriately wreathed in time, dating from a Battle of the Flowers in 1890 which also incorporated a mock Roman Chariot Race. This proved to be too dangerous with the subsequent substitution of a football game in 1916.

Just in case it all gets too serious, the good folk of Pasadena like to take the mickey out of the Rose Parade with an annual, November Doo Dah Parade, which is a form of synchronised madness. The participants in this parade show rare ingenuity with their entries. One gentleman completely swathed in bandages marches by himself, allegedly at the head of the Claude Raines Invisible Marching Band, a precision drill team of suited

Outskirts

business men and women carrying brief cases perform like a gung-ho corps of Marines, a group of dapper 'British' executives in pin stripes and carrying furled umbrellas similarly parade while the oddest looking are a group of marchers dressed as hamburgers.

However, for most of the year, the residents patronise the serious arts.

An excellent collection of Early American, European and Asian art is at the **Norton Simon Museum** at 411 W. Colorado Boulevard. The museum is named for the wealthy businessman who devoted his energies to revamping the former collection in the city and adding many new and significant works. The museum however is only open for limited hours so it is wise to check before making the journey. If your taste is solely Asian you may be more interested in the **Pacific Asian Museum** at 46 N. Los Robles Avenue, where the collection is devoted purely to the crafts and arts of Asia and the Pacific islands.

The small **Pasadena Santa Fe Railroad Station** on South Raymond Avenue is a fine example of Reproduction Spanish Colonial Architecture. During the 'Golden Years' of Hollywood it was a major stopping place for movie stars

Long Beach, Queen Mary

Outskirts

and studio executives who travelled from the east on the famous 'Super Chief' or the 'Twentieth Century Limited'. Rather than face the waiting Press at Union Station in Downtown L.A., especially if they were with a partner they shouldn't be with, the stars would alight here to waiting limousines and be taken to their homes in Beverly Hills. Of course the Press soon woke up to this trick but the disembarkation at Pasadena still took place as a publicity stunt.

The Spanish style was also used in the construction of the **Pasadena Playhouse** at 39 South El Molina Avenue. It was the training ground for stars like William Holden, Tyrone Power and Raymond Burr. It has been refurbished and still provides top theatrical productions providing a venue for those stars who still miss the atmosphere of working to a live audience.

Pasadena has also produced the prestigious **California Institute of Technology** whose high-tech. work has generated a nice shelf of Nobel Prizes.

Pasadena is not an essential on the tour itinerary being of more interest to the local Angelenos. However if you have time to kill and a car at your disposal you can spend an amiable day pottering around.

The Queen Mary and Dome

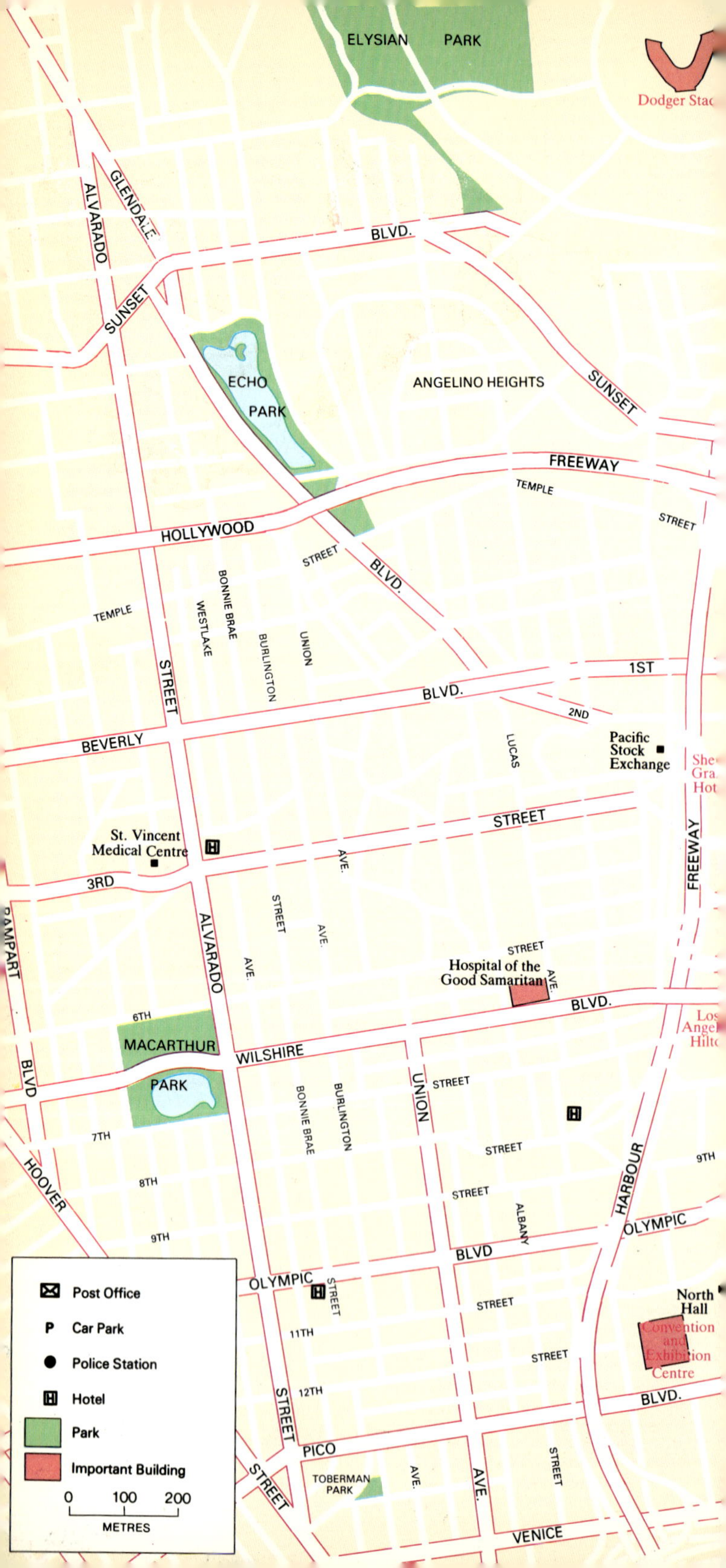

ELYSIAN PARK
Dodger Stad
GLENDALE
ALVARADO
BLVD.
SUNSET
ECHO PARK
ANGELINO HEIGHTS
SUNSET
FREEWAY
TEMPLE
STREET
HOLLYWOOD
STREET
BLVD.
TEMPLE
BONNIE BRAE
WESTLAKE
BURLINGTON
UNION
STREET
1ST
BLVD.
2ND
BEVERLY
LUCAS
Pacific Stock Exchange
She Gra Hot
STREET
St. Vincent Medical Centre
3RD
AVE.
FREEWAY
RAMPART
STREET
AVE.
AVE.
ALVARADO
STREET
Hospital of the Good Samaritan
AVE.
BLVD.
6TH
MACARTHUR PARK
WILSHIRE
Los Angel Hilto
BLVD
BONNIE BRAE
BURLINGTON
UNION
STREET
7TH
HOOVER
8TH
STREET
STREET
9TH
ALBANY
HARBOUR
9TH
OLYMPIC
9TH
BLVD
OLYMPIC
STREET
STREET
North Hall
Convention and Exhibition Centre
11TH
STREET
12TH
BLVD.
STREET
PICO
STREET
TOBERMAN PARK
AVE.
AVE.
STREET
VENICE
Post Office
Car Park
Police Station
Hotel
Park
Important Building
0 100 200
METRES

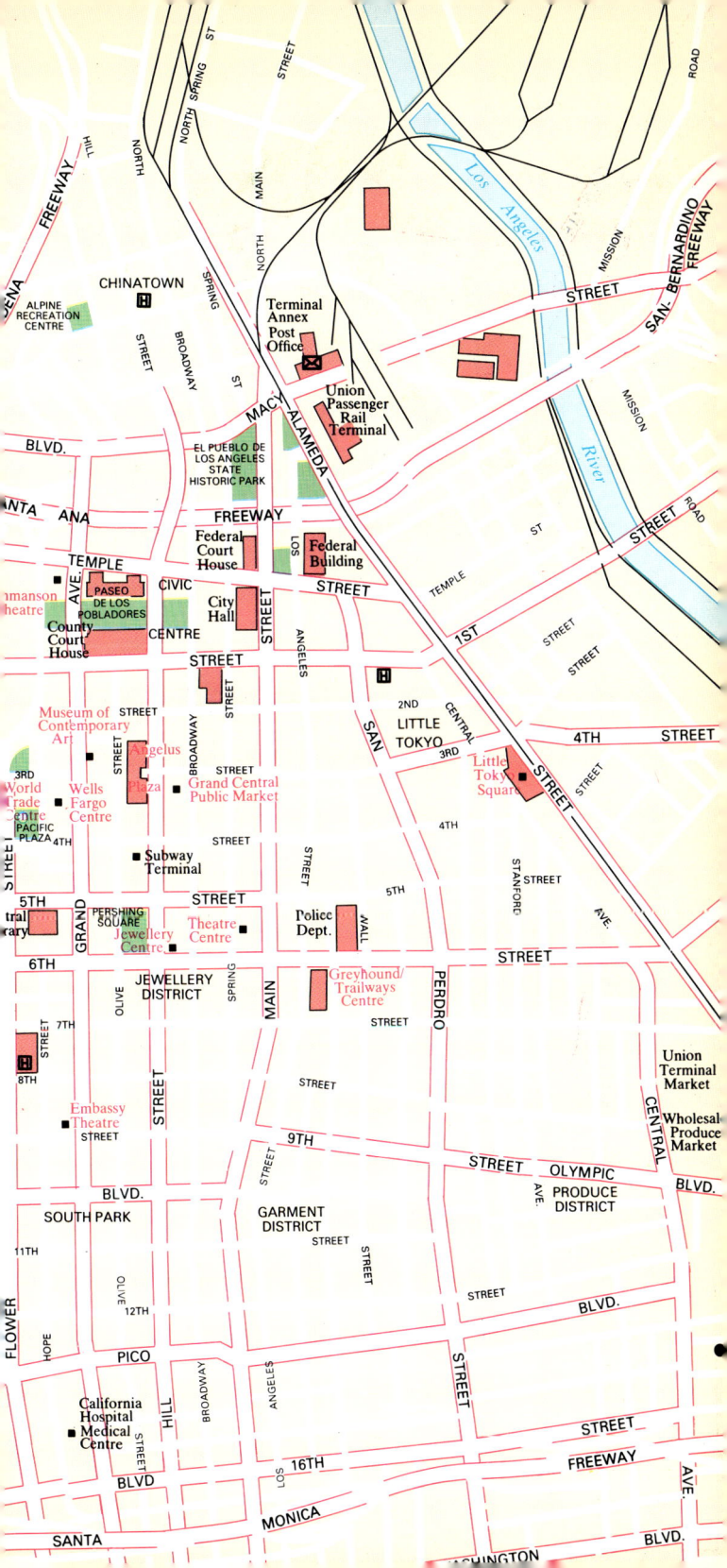

Streets and Landmarks (Downtown Los Angeles Map)

Freeways / Major Roads:
- PASADENA FREEWAY
- SANTA ANA FREEWAY
- SAN BERNARDINO FREEWAY
- HOLLYWOOD FREEWAY
- SANTA MONICA BLVD.
- WASHINGTON BLVD.
- OLYMPIC BLVD.
- PICO BLVD.
- MISSION ROAD

Streets:
- HILL STREET
- NORTH SPRING STREET
- NORTH MAIN STREET
- NORTH BROADWAY
- NORTH SPRING ST
- MACY STREET
- ALAMEDA STREET
- TEMPLE STREET
- 1ST STREET
- 2ND STREET
- 3RD STREET
- 4TH STREET
- 5TH STREET
- 6TH STREET
- 7TH STREET
- 8TH STREET
- 9TH STREET
- 11TH STREET
- 12TH STREET
- 16TH STREET
- FLOWER STREET
- HOPE STREET
- GRAND AVE.
- OLIVE STREET
- BROADWAY
- SPRING STREET
- MAIN STREET
- LOS ANGELES STREET
- SAN PEDRO STREET
- CENTRAL AVE.
- STANFORD STREET
- MALL

Landmarks:
- ALPINE RECREATION CENTRE
- CHINATOWN
- Terminal Annex Post Office
- Union Passenger Rail Terminal
- EL PUEBLO DE LOS ANGELES STATE HISTORIC PARK
- PASEO DE LOS POBLADORES
- Federal Court House
- Federal Building
- City Hall
- CIVIC CENTRE
- County Court House
- Mark Taper Theatre (Ahmanson Theatre)
- Museum of Contemporary Art
- World Trade Centre
- PACIFIC PLAZA
- Angelus Plaza
- Wells Fargo Centre
- Grand Central Public Market
- Subway Terminal
- Central Library
- PERSHING SQUARE
- Jewellery Centre
- Theatre Centre
- Police Dept.
- Little Tokyo Square
- LITTLE TOKYO
- JEWELLERY DISTRICT
- Greyhound/Trailways Centre
- Embassy Theatre
- Union Terminal Market
- Wholesale Produce Market
- PRODUCE DISTRICT
- GARMENT DISTRICT
- SOUTH PARK
- California Hospital Medical Centre
- Los Angeles River

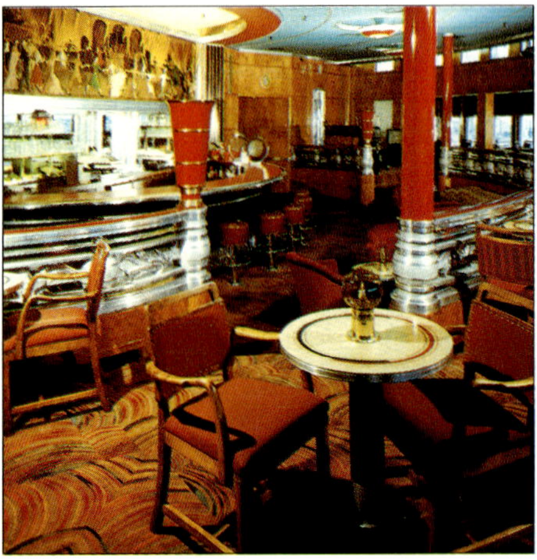

PART III
Accommodation

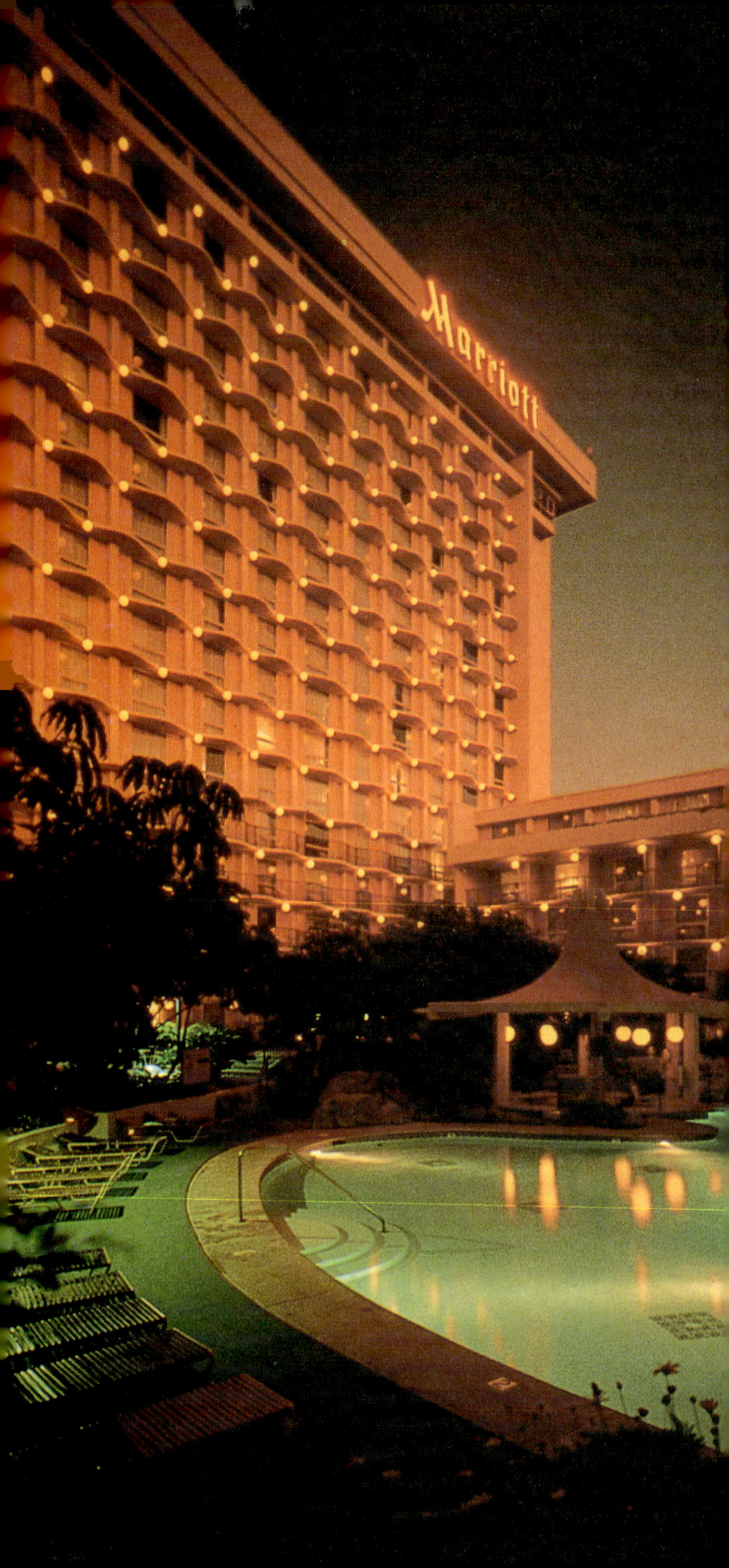
Marriott

HOTELS-MOTELS

General Notes

At first glance, L.A.'s size and diversity may seem overwhelming. In fact, it is a series of unique towns, communites and neighbourhoods. This guide organises accommodations by regions such as 'Downtown', 'Hollywood', and so forth.

1) Room rates are applicable daily, and are usually up to 11 am of the following day. They are quoted in U.S. dollars and may be subject to city, county or state taxes.
2) To ensure accommodation in the hotel or motel of your choice, a reservations are highly recommended. Most hotels require a deposit equal to one night's stay or a credit card number. Without a deposit or credit card guarantee, rooms will generally not be held after 6pm.
3) Single room rates refer to the price for one person in one room. In a double, two people can occupy a room which may have only one bed. If two beds are required ask the hotel for a 'twin' or a 'double-double' room. Consult individual properties for special family rates.

> **INFOTIP:** Toll free numbers connect visitors free of charge to the hotel reservations centres.

Legend

AC - Air Conditioning
G - Golf
R - Restaurant
TEL - Telephone
TV - Television/Video
T - Tennis Court
RM - Room Service
CL - Coctail Lounge
CAB - Courtesy Airport Bus
SP - Swimming Pool
FE - Foreign Exchange
J - Jacuzzi
FT - Free Transportation within Downtown
B - Babysitting
RF - Refrigerator in room
MP - Most Pets

Accommodation

First class bathroom, Queen Mary

DOWNTOWN

BUDGET INN MOTEL
1710 W. 7th Street
Los Angeles CA 90017
Tel.(213) 483 3470
TV, TEL, SP, R, CAB, TEL

CITY CENTRE MOTEL
1135 W. 7th Street
Los Angeles CA 90017
Tel.(213) 628 7141
TEL, AC, CAB, RM, SP, R, CL

COMFORT INN TOWNE
4122 S. Western
Los Angeles CA 90062
Tel.(213) 294 5200
TV, TEL, AC, J

THE DOWNTOWNER MOTEL
944 S. Georgia Street
Los Angeles CA 90015
Tel.(213) 627 2003
TV, AC, TEL, SP, CAB, R, CL

Accommodation

EXECUTIVE FRIENDSHIP INN
457 S. Mariposa Avenue
Los Angeles CA 90020
Tel.(213) 380 6910
Toll.(800) 453 4511
J, SM, TV, TEL, RM

FIGUEROA HOTEL
939 S. Figueroa Street
Los Angeles CA 90015
Tel.(213) 627 8971
Toll.(800) 421 9092
CAB, R, CL, SM, J, T, G, TEL

HUNTINGTON HOTEL
752 S. Main Street
Los Angeles CA 90014
Tel.(213) 627 3186
CL, CAB, TEL

HYATT REGENCY LOS ANGELES
711 S. Hope Street
Los Angeles CA 90017
Tel.(213) 683 1234
Toll.(800) 233 1234
CAB, R, CL, RM, J, B, MP,
FF, SP, T, G, TEL

MILNER HOTEL
813 S. Flower Street
Los Angeles CA 90017
Tel.(213) 627 6981
Toll.(800) 521 0592
R, CL, CAB, TEL

ORCHID HOTEL
819 S. Flower Street
Los Angeles CA 90017
Tel.(213) 624 5855
CAB, R, TEL

SHERATON GRANDE HOTEL
333 S. Figueroa Street
Los Angeles CA 90071
Tel.(213) 617 1133
Toll.(800) 325 3535
CAB, R, CL, RM, SP, B, FE,
TEL, J, T, G

HYATT WILSHIRE
3515 Wilshire Blvd
Los Angeles CA 90010
Tel.(213) 381 7411
Toll.(800) 233 1234
T, G, CAB, R, CL, RM, SP,
B, FE, TEL, J

JERRY'S MOTEL
285 S. Lucas Avenue
Los Angeles CA 90026
Tel.(213) 481 0921
TV, RM, CAB, R, SP, T, TEL

LOS ANGELES HILTON AND TOWERS
930 Wilshire Blvd
Los Angeles CA 90017
Tel.(213) 629 4321
Toll.(800) 445 8667
R, SP, CAB, CL, RM,
B, FE, T, TEL

LOS ANGELES INN
1240 W. 7th Street
Los Angeles CA 90017
Tel.(213) 626 3590
TEL, TV, R, CAB

PARK PLAZA HOTEL
607 S. Park View Street
Los Angeles CA 90057
Tel.(213) 384 5281
R, CL, SP, J, B, CAB, T

ROYAL HOST OLYMPIC MOTEL
901 W. Olympic Blvd
Los Angeles CA 90015
Tel.(213) 626 6255
AC, TEL, TV, R, CAB

SHERATON TOWN HOUSE
2961 Wilshire Blvd
Los Angeles CA 90010
Tel.(213) 382 7171
Toll.(800) 325 3535
CAB, R, CL, RM, SP,
T, B, FE, J, G, TEL

Accommodation

STILLWELL HOTEL
838 S. Grand Avenue
Los Angeles CA 90017
Tel.(213) 627 1151
Toll.(800) 553 4774
AC, TV, TEL, RF, R, CL, RM, MP

UNIVERSITY HILTON
3540 S. Figueroa Street
Los Angeles CA 90007
Tel.(213) 748 4141
Toll.(800) 445 8667
R, CAB, CL, RM, SP, J, B, FE, T, TEL

USC SUMMER CONFERENCES
642 W. 34th Street
Los Angeles CA 900891332
Tel.(213) 743 2022
CL, SP, T, CAB, R, TEL

WHILSHIRE COMFORT INN
3400 W. Third Street
Los Angeles CA 90020
Tel.(213) 385 0061
Toll.(800) 228 5050
TV, TEL, R, RM, SP, J, T, G

WILSHIRE ROYALE HOTEL
2619 Wilshire Blvd
Los Angeles CA 90057
Tel.(213) 387 5311
Toll.(800) 421 8072
R, CL, SP, J, CAB, TEL, T

VERMONT MOTEL
1717 S. Vermont Avenue
Los Angeles CA 90006
Tel.(213) 730 1578
AC, TEL, TV, J

HOLLYWOOD

BEVONSHIRE LODGE MOTEL
7575 Beverly Blvd
Los Angeles CA 90036
Tel.(213) 936 6154
TV, AC, TEL, CAB, SP, B,
R, CL, J, T, G

CONSORT LEGACY HOTEL
1160 N. Vermont Avenue
Hollywood CA 90029
Tel.(213) 660 1788
Toll.(800) 346 4974
CAB, R, CL, RM, SP, J, T, G, TEL

**DUNES WILSHIRE
MOTEL HOTEL**
4300 Wilshire Blvd
Los Angeles CA 90010
Tel.(213) 938 3616
Toll.(800) 452 3863
CAB, R, CL, RM, SP, J, T, G, B

HASTINGS HOTEL
6162 Hollywood Blvd
Hollywood CA 90028
Tel.(213) 464 4136
SP, J, T, G, TEL

HIGHLAND GARDENS HOTEL
7047 Franklin Avenue
Los Angeles CA 90028
Tel.(213) 850 0536
SP, CAB, R, CL, J, T, G, TEL

**HOLLYWOOD ROOSEVELT
HOTEL**
7000 Hollywood Blvd
Hollywood CA 90028
Tel.(213) 466 7000
Toll.(800) 950 7667
CAB, R, CL, RM, SP, J, B,
FE, T, G, TEL

HOLLYWOOD VINE MOTEL
1133 Vine Street
Hollywood CA 90038
Tel.(213) 466 7501
AC, TV, SP, CAB, TEL

HYATT ON SUNSET
8401 Sunset Blvd
Hollywood CA 90069
Tel.(213) 656 1234
Toll.(800) 228 9000
CAB, R, CL, RM, SP, FE, J, TEL

Accommodation

LE DUFY HOTEL
1000 Westmont Drive
West Hollywood CA 90069
Tel.(213) 657 7400
Toll.(800) 424 4443
RM, SP, J, B, FE, R, CL, T, G, TEL

LE PARC HOTEL
733 N. West Knoll
West Hollywood CA 90069
Tel.(213) 855 8888
Toll.(800) 424 4443
Fax.(213) 659 7812
R, CL, RM, SP, J, T, B, G, TEL

LE REVE HOTEL
8822 Cynthia Street
West Hollywood CA 90069
Tel.(213) 854 1114
Toll.(800) 424 4443
Fax.(213)854 0926
RM, SP, J, FE, T, G, TEL

LOS ANGELES MIDTOWN HILTON
400 N. Vermont
Los Angeles CA 90004
Tel.(213) 662 4888
TV, R, CAB, R, CL, RM, B, T, G, TEL

SAHARAN MOTOR HOTEL
7212 Sunset Blvd
Hollywood CA 90046
Tel.(213) 874 6700
CAB, R

ST JAMES'S CLUB
8358 Sunset Blvd
Los Angeles CA 90069
Tel.(213) 654 7100
Toll.(800) 225 2637
R, CL, RM, SP, J, B, FE, CAB, T, G, TEL

ST MORITZ HOTEL
5849 Sunset Blvd
Hollywood CA 90028
Tel.(213) 467 2174
TEL, CL, CAB, R

MONDRIAN HOTEL
8440 Sunset Blvd
West Hollywood CA 90069
Tel.(213) 650 8999
Toll.(800) 424 4443
Fax.(213) 650 5215
R, CL, RM, SP, J, B, FE, T, G, TEL

PARK PLAZA LODGE
6001 W. 3rd Street
Los Angeles CA 90036
Tel.(213) 931 1501
R, CL, RM, SP, J, T, TEL

THE REGISTRY HOTEL - LOS ANGELES
555 Universal Terrace Parkway
Universal City
Los Angeles CA 91608-1095
Tel.(818) 506 2500
Toll.(800) 247 9801
CAB, R, CL, RM, SP, J, B, T, G, T

RODEWAY INN HOLLYWOOD
7023 W. Sunset Blvd
Hollywood CA 90028
Tel.(213) 464 8344
Toll.(800) 255 7249
TEL, TV, R, SP, J, CAB

SUNSET PLAZA HOTEL
8400 Sunset Blvd
Los Angeles CA 90069
Tel.(213) 654 0750
Toll.(800) 421 3652
CAB, SP, T, G, TEL

VALADON HOTEL
900 Hammond Street
West Hollywood CA 90069
Tel.(213) 855 1115
Toll.(800)424 4443
SP, J, T, R, RM, B, FE, TEL, CL, G

BEL AGE HOTEL
1020 N. San Vincente Blvd
West Hollywood CA 90069
Tel.(213) 854 1111
Toll.(800) 424 4443
TV, TEL, R, CL, RM, SP, J, FE
T, G, B

Accommodation

WESTSIDE

THE BEL-AIR SUMMIT HOTEL
11461 Sunset Blvd
Los Angeles CA 90049
Tel.(213) 476 6571
Toll.(800) 421 6649
RF, TEL, AC, R, CL, RM, SP,
T, B, CAB, G

THE BEVERLY HILTON
9876 Wilshire Blvd
Beverly Hills CA 90210
Tel.(213) 274 7777
Toll.(800) 445 8667
CAB, R, CL, RM, SP, B, MP,
FE, T, G, TEL

BEVERLY HILLS HOTEL
9641 Sunset Blvd
Beverly Hills CA 90210
Tel.(213) 276 2251
Toll.(800) 792 7637
T, R, CL, RM, SP, J, B, FE,
CAB, G, TEL

BEVERLY PAVILION HOTEL
9360 Wilshire Blvd
Beverly Hills CA 90212
Tel.(213) 273 1400
Toll.(800) 421 0545
R, CL, RM, SP, B,
CAB, J, T, G, TEL

BEVERLY PLAZA HOTEL
8384 W. Third Street
Los Angeles CA 90048
Tel.(213) 658 6600
Toll.(800) 624 6835
R, CL, RM, SP, J, B,
CAB, T, G, TEL

L'ERMITAGE HOTEL
9291 Burton Way
Beverly Hills CA 90210
Tel.(213) 278 3344
Toll.(800) 424 4443
R, CL, RM, SP, J, B,
FE, T, G, TEL

Sitting room, first class, Queen Mary

Accommodation

MA MAISON SOFITEL
8555 Beverly Blvd
Los Angeles CA 90048
Tel.(213) 278 5444
Toll.(800) 221 4542
CAB, R, CL, RM, SP, B,
MP, FE, J, T, G, TEL

MAGIC HOTEL
7025 Franklin Avenue
Hollywood CA 90068
Tel.(213) 851 0800
TEL, TV, CAB, SP, MP

**RAMADA HOTEL
- BEVERLY HILLS**
1150 S. Beverly Drive
Los Angeles CA 90035
Tel. (213) 553 6561
Toll.(800) 272 6232
CAB, R, CL, RM, SP,
J, T, G, TEL

**RAMADA WEST
HOLLYWOOD**
8585 Santa Monica Blvd
West hollywood CA 90069
Tel.(213) 652 5720
Toll.(800) 228 2828
CAB, R, CL, RM, SP, B, FE,
J, T, G, TEL

CENTURY PLAZA HOTEL & TOWER
2025 Avenue of the Stars
Los Angeles CA 90067
Tel.(213) 277 2000
Toll.(800) 228 3000
TEL, FT, CAB, R, CL, RM, SP, J,
MP, FE, T, G, B

CENTURY WILSHIRE HOTEL
10776 Wilshire Blvd
Los Angeles CA 90024
Tel.(213) 474 4506
Toll.(800) 421 7223
SP, TEL

CREST MOTEL
7701 Beverly Blvd
Los Angeles CA 90036
Tel.(213) 931 8108
Toll.(800) 367 1717
TEL, TV, SP, R, CL

**JW MARRIOTT HOTEL
AT CENTURY CITY**
2151 Avenue of the Stars
Los Angeles CA 90067
Tel.(213) 277 2777
Toll.(800) 228 9290
SP, R, CL, RM, B, FE,
CAB, T, G, TEL

COASTAL

BAYVIEW PLAZA HOLIDAY INN
530 Pico Blvd
Santa Monica CA 90405
Tel.(213) 399 9344
Toll.(800) 465 4329
J, R, CL, RM, SP, FE, T, B, TEL

EL TOVAR BY THE SEA
603 Ocean Avenue
Santa Monica CA 90402
Tel.(213) 451 1820
CAB, R, RM, B, SP, J, T, G, TEL

**GUEST QUARTERS SUITE
HOTEL - SANTA MONICA**
1723 Fourth Street
Santa Monica CA 90401
Toll.(800) 424 2900
R, CL, RM, SP, J, CAB, T, G, TEL

SHANGRI-LA HOTEL
1301 Ocean Avenue
Santa Monica CA 90401
Tel.(213) 394 2791
CAB, R, CL, SP, J, T, G, TEL

Accommodation

**THE SOVERIEGN
AT SANTA MONICA BAY**
205 Washington Avenue
Santa Monica CA 90403
Tel.(213) 395 9921
Toll.(800) 331 0163
CAB, B, R, CL, SP, J, T, G, TEL

PACIFIC SHORE HOTEL
1819 Ocean Avenue
Santa Monica CA 90401
Tel.(213) 451 8711
Toll.(800) 241 3848
R, CL, RM, SP, J, B,
FE, T, G, TEL

**SANTA MONICA
TRAVELODGE**
1525 Ocean Avenue
Santa Monica CA 90401
Tel.(213) 451 0761
Toll.(800) 255 3050
SP, CAB, TEL

HUNTLEY HOTEL
1111 Second Street
Santa Monica CA 90403
Tel.(213) 394 5454
Toll.(800) 556 4011
R, CAB, CL, RM, B, SP,
J, T, G, TEL

HOTEL SANTA MONICA
3102 Pico Blvd
Santa Monica CA 90405
Tel.(213) 450 5766
Toll.(800) 231 7679
CAB, SP, J, T, G, TEL

**MIRAMARA-SHERATON
HOTEL**
101 Wilshire Blvd
Santa Monica CA 90401
Tel.(213) 394 3731
Toll.(800) 325 3535
CAB, R, CL, RM, SP, B,
FE, J, T, G, TEL

MARINA DEL REY, VENICE

**DOUBLE TREE HOTEL-
MARINA DEL REY**
4100 Admiralty Way
Marina del Rey CA 90292
Tel.(213) 301 3000
Toll.(800) 882 4000
CAB, R, CL, RM, SP, B, TEL

THE FOGHORN HOTEL
4140 Via Marina
Marina del Rey CA 90292
Tel.(213) 823 4626
Toll.(800) 423 4940
CAB, R, CL, MP, J, T, TEL

**VENICE BEACH
HOTEL/MOTEL**
25 Windard Avenue
Venice CA 90291
Tel.(213) 399 7649
CAB, R, CL, RM, TEL

FOLKS-TEL
15 Paloma Avenue
Venice CA 90291
Tel.(213) 392 7039
CAB, R, TEL

MARINA DEL REY HOTEL
13534 Bali Way
Marina Del Rey CA 90292
Tel.(213) 301 1000
Toll.(800) 882 4000
CAB, R, CL, RM, SP,
B, T, G, TEL

MARINA DEL REY MARRIOTT
13480 Maxella Avenue
Marina Del Rey CA 90292
Tel.(213) 822 8555
Toll.(800) 228 9290
CAB, R, CL, RM, SP, J, B,
MP, FE, T, G, TEL

Accommodation

Strolling at the Marina Del Rey

Dusk at Fisherman's Village

Accommodation

AIRPORT AREA

AIRPORT MARINA HOTEL
8601 Lincoln Blvd
Los Angeles CA 90045
Tel.(213) 670 8111
Toll.(800) 227 1117
FT, CAB, R, CL, RM, SP,
FE, J, T, G, TEL

AIRPORT COURTESY INN
901 W. Manchester Blvd
Inglewood CA 90301
Tel.(213) 649 0800
Toll.(800) 231 2508
CAB, R, SP, CL, T, G, TEL

**BEST WESTERN
AIRPORT PLAZA INN**
1730 Centinela Avenue
Inglewood CA 90302
Tel.(213) 568 0071
Toll.(800) 528 1234
TV, CAB, SP, J, R, CL

CAPRI MOTEL
8620 Airport Blvd
Los Angeles CA 90045
Tel.(213) 645 7700
TEL, TV, CAB, SP, B,
R, CL, J, T, G

THE COCKATOO INN
4334 W. Imperial Highway
Hawthorne CA 90250
Tel.(213) 679 2291
Toll.(800) 262 5286
FT, CAB, R, CL, RM, SP,
B, J, T, G, TEL

DAYS INN LAX
5101 Century Blvd
Inglewood CA 90304
Tel.(213) 673 2311
Toll.(800) 325 2525
SP, CAB, R, CL, RM, SP, TEL

GENEVA BUDGET MOTEL
321 W. Manchester Blvd
Inglewood CA 90301
Tel.(213) 677 9171
TEL, TV, CAB, R, CL,
SP, J, T, G, TEL

HACIENDA HOTEL
525 N. Sepulevda Blvd
El Segundo CA 90245
Tel.(213) 615 0015
Toll.(800) 421 5900
TV, CAB, R, CL, RM,
SP, J, T, G, TEL

Accommodation

HOLIDAY INN CROWNE PLAZA
5985 Century Blvd
Los Angeles CA 90045
Tel.(213) 642 7500
Toll.(800) 465 4329
CAB, R, CL, RM, SP,
B, J, T, G, TEL

HOLIDAY INN-LAX
9901 S. La Cienega Blvd
Los Angeles CA 90045
Tel.(213) 649 5151
Toll.(800) 465 4329
CAB, R, CL, RM, SP,
B, FE, TEL

HYATT AT LOS ANGELES AIRPORT
6225 W. Century Blvd
Los Angeles CA 90045
Tel.(213) 670 9000
Toll.(800) 233 1234
TV, CAB, R, CL, RM, SP,
B, MP, J, T, G, TEL

LAX HOTEL
1804 E. Sycamore
El Segundo CA 90245
Tel.(213) 615 0133
Toll.(800) 421 5781
CAB, TV, SP, J, T, G

LOS ANGELES AIRPORT HILTON & TOWERS
5711 W. Century Blvd
Los Angeles CA 90045
Tel.(213) 410 4000
Toll.(800) 445 8667
CAB, R, CL, RM, SP, J,
B, MP, FE, T, G, TEL

LOS ANGELES AIRPORT MARRIOTT HOTEL
5855 W. Century Blvd
Los Angeles CA 90045
Tel.(213) 641 5700
Toll.(800) 228 9290
TV, CAB, R, CL, RM, SP,
J, B, MP, FE, T, G, TEL

LOYOLA MARYMOUNT UNIVERSITY
Loyola Blvd at W. 80th Street
Los Angeles CA 90045
Tel.(213) 642 2975
R, SP, J, T, B, G, TEL

PACIFICA HOTEL & CONFERENCE CENTRE
6161 Centinela Avenue
Culver City CA 90230
Tel.(213) 649 1776
Toll.(800) 854 2608
CAB, FT, R, CL, RM,
SP, J, T, G, TEL

QUALITY INN HOTEL AT LOS ANGELES AIRPORT
5249 W. Century Blvd
Los Angeles CA 90045
Tel.(213) 645 2200
Toll.(800) 228 5151
R, CL, CAB, RM, SP,
B, T, G, TEL

RAMADA HOTEL CULVER CITY
6333 Bristol Parkway
Culver City CA 90230
Tel.(213) 670 3200
Toll.(800) 272 6232
CAB, R, CL, RM, SP,
J, B, T, G, TEL

RAMADA INN INTERNATIONAL AIRPORT
9620 Airport Blvd
Los Angeles CA 90045
Tel.(213) 670 1600
Toll.(800) 228 2828
CAB, R, RM, SP, T, G, TEL

SHERATON PLAZA LA REINA HOTEL
6101 W. Century Blvd
Los Angeles CA 90045
Tel.(213) 642 1111
Toll.(800) 325 3535
TV, CAB, R, CL, RM, SP,
J, B, MP, FE, T, G, TEL

Accommodation

SOUTH BAY AND BEACH CITIES

AT OCEAN MOTEL
50 Atlantic Avenue
Long Beach CA 90802
Tel.(213) 435 8369
TV, RF, TEL, MP, CAB,
R, CL, SP, T, G

HOLIDAY INN TORRANCE/ HARBOR GATEWAY
19800 S. Vermont Avenue
Torrance CA 90502
Tel.(213)781 9100
Toll.(800) 465 4329
R, CL, RM, SP, J, B,
CAB, T, G, TEL

QUEEN MARY HOTEL
Pier J
P.O. Box 8
Long Beach CA 90801
Tel.(213) 435 3511
Toll.(800) 421 3732
CAB, R, CL, RM, B, FE,
T, G, TEL

ROYAL PACIFIC INN
850 N. Sepulveda Blvd
Manhattan Beach CA 90266
Tel.(213) 318 1020
Toll.(800) 627 7466
TV, CAB, SP, J, R, CL, TEL.

SEA SPRITE OCEAN FRONT AP. MOTEL
1016 Strand
Hermosa Beach CA 90254
Tel. (213) 376 6933
TV, SP, B, CL, T, G, TEL

SHERATON AT REDONDO BEACH
300 N. Harbor Drive
Redondo Beach CA 90277
Tel. (213) 318 8888
Toll (800) 325 3535
CAB, R, CL, RM, SP, J, T,
B, FE, G, TEL

TORRANCE MARRIOTT HOTEL
3635 Fashion Way
Torrance CA 90503
Tel. (213) 316 3636
Toll. (800) 228 9290
R, CL, RM, SP, J, B, FE,
CAB, T, G, TEL

BEST WESTERN SOUTH BAY HOTEL
15000 Hawthorne Blvd
Lawndale CA 90260
Tel.(213) 973 0998
Toll.(800) 528 1234
CAB, R, CL, SP, J, B, MP, TEL

THE VALLEYS

BELAIR-BED & BREAKFAST
941 N. Frederic Avenue
Burbank CA 91505
Tel. (818) 848 9227
RM, B, CAB, R, CL,
SP, J, T, G, TEL

BURBANK AIRPORT HILTON
2500 Hollywood Way
Burbank CA 91505
Tel. (818) 843 6000
CAB, R, CL, RM, SP, J, B,
MP, FE, T, G, TEL

DISNEYLAND HOTEL
1150 W. Cerritos Avenue
Anaheim CA 92802
Tel. (714) 778 6600
CAB, R, CL, RM, SP,
T, B, FE, J, G, TEL

GRANADA INN OF ANAHEIM
2375 W. Lincoln Avenue
Anaheim CA 92801
Tel. (714) 774 7370
Toll. (800) 648 8685
R, SP, B, CAB, T, G, TEL

Accommodation

WARNER CENTER HILTON
6360 Canoga Avenue
Woodland Hills CA 91367
Tel. (818) 595 1000
Toll. (800) 445 8667
CAB, R, CL, RM, B,
SP, J, T, G, TEL

**WARNER CENTER
MARRIOTT WOODLAND HILLS**
21850 Oxnard Street
Woodland Hills CA 91367
Tel. (818) 887 4800
Toll. (800) 228 9290
CAB, R, CL, RM, SP, J, B,
MP, FE, T, G, TEL

**BEST WESTERN
COURTESY INN**
1200 S. West
Anaheim CA 92802
Tel. (714) 722 2470
Toll. (800) 528 1234
SP, J, CAB, R, CL, T, TEL

**HOLIDAY INN
PASADENA CONV. CENTER**
303 E. Cordova Street
Pasadena CA 91101
Tel. (818) 449 4000
Toll.(800) 238 8000
CAB, R, CL, RM, SP,
T, B, MP, G, TEL

Tomorrowland, Disney

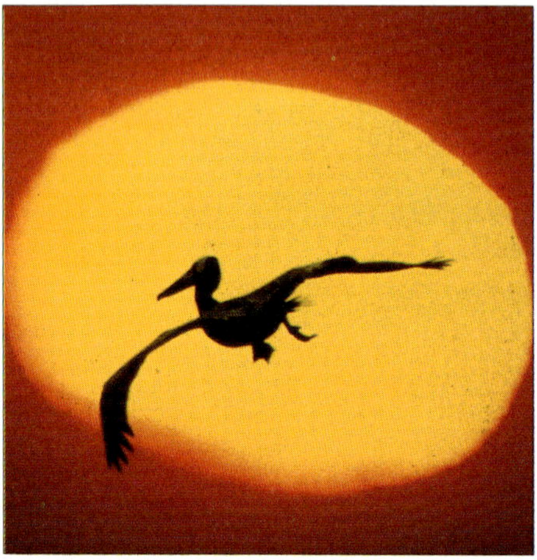

PART IV
Practical Information

PRACTICAL INFORMATION

ADVANCE PLANNING	139
CRIME	155
ELECTRICITY	142
ENTERTAINMENT	142
Art Galleries	142
Children's Entertainment	143
Casinos and Card Clubs	143
Cinema	143
ENTRY REGULATIONS	139
Customs	140
Concessions for all Travellers	140
Live Animals	140
Plants	140
Currency	141
FESTIVALS AND PUBLIC HOLIDAYS	144
GETTING AROUND LOS ANGELES	148
GETTING OUTSIDE LOS ANGELES	151
GETTING TO LOS ANGELES	141
HELP	151
Consulates	152
Medical Emergencies	153
Police Emergencies	153
Death	153
Lost Property	154
Replacement of Certain Items	154
Information for disabled people	154
LIBRARIES	157
MOTORING	155
Traffic Laws	155
Parking	155
In Case of Accident	156
Rental Cars	156
MUSIC/ORCHESTRAS/CONCERTS	146
POST OFFICE	157
RADIO/TELEVISION	148
RELIGIOUS SERVICES	158
RESTAURANTS AND NIGHTLIFE	158
Nightclubs	158
Restaurants	161
Dinner Theatres	168
SHOPPING	169
SPORTS AND ATHLETICS	172
TELEPHONES AND TELEGRAMS	176
THE METRIC SYSTEM	178
THEATRE	146

TIME	177
TOURS AND CRUISES	177
TOURIST SERVICES	178
THE METRIC SYSTEM	178

Californian Skiing

Advance Planning

What to bring

Documents:
  Passport, all major credit cards - including Discover Card and Japan Credit Bureau, International drivers licence, student card.

Clothing:
  The emphasis is on the casual, only some restaurants require jackets and ties for men. You will, however, find a sweater or lightweight jacket comfortable since most evenings are cool. Although casual, Los Angeles is also the perfect place to wear the one-of-a-kind outfit you save for special occasions.
  The city still clings to its clothing traditions when it comes to business, so that means suits and ties. Shorts and long socks are acceptable in some organisations. A jacket may be required by international-class hotels in their premier dinning rooms.
  But in general, Los Angeles requires light and casual clothes.

Medical Tips:
  Check with your insurance company to see if you are covered while travelling. Make a note of generic names of prescription drugs incase of loss ask a pharmacist for advise. If you suffer from chronic illness it is a good idea to carry a note from your doctor, outlining drugs you are taking and any necessary further treatment incase of relapse.

> **INFOTIP:** Dress for the district you are visiting. If going to the less respectable parts of Downtown L.A. don't dress like a flashy tourist. Similarly if you dress like a bum whilst wandering around Beverly Hills and Bel Air you will find yourself being stopped by the local security patrols.

Entry Regulations

The right documents for a visit to United States are: a valid passport and a visitor's visa. Your visa can be obtained

Practical Information

by personal application to the U.S. Embassy or Consulate nearest to you.

A passport size photograph and valid evidence that you intend to leave the United States after your visit will be required.

British subjects residing in Canada or Bermuda are normally exempt from these requirements. Also exempt are citizens of Mexico with form 1-186 travelling from Canada or Mexico.

Customs

Your entry into the United States will be simpler and quicker if you prepare the documents provided en route to U.S. by airline or ship personnel.

Concessions for all Travellers

Any traveller may bring the following articles into the United States without paying any duty on them as long as the articles accompanies you through Customs and are not intended for commercial purposes:

Alcohol: 1 litre of alcoholic liquor, including wine, beer or spirits per person over 18 years og age, local state laws permitting.

Tobacco: 200 cigarettes, or 50 cigars, 3 pounds of tabacco (1.63 Kilos) or proportionate amounts of each.

Gifts: to the value of $100.00 US providing you intend to remain in the United States for more than 72 hours. Alcoholic beverages and tabacco are not included.

Clothings: All personal clothing, including toiletries and jewelry.

Sporting equipment and miscellaneous goods: such as cameras, portable radio, binoculars, wheelchair etc, provided that they are not intended for commercial pruposes.

Live Animals

Pets are subject to health agriculture and customs requirements at the port of entry. As local rules and regulations at your final destination in the United States vary. Check at your Embassy or Consulate for exact details.

Plants

Any plants, fruits, vegetables or seeds will not be allowed in the United States without special permission. If in any doubt inquire at your Embassy or Consulate. Such items must be declared at the port of entry.

Practical Information

LAX at Dusk

Currency

Amounts in excess of $5,000 US dollars must be declared on arrival.

> **INFOTIP:** Railway, bus and air terminals in the United States sell accident insurance policies on individual journeys. These can be bought from the insurance counters or vending machines.

GETTING TO LOS ANGELES

By Rail. Trains are usually cheaper than airplanes over short distances and get you from city centre to city centre. AMTRAK (America's National Railroad Passenger Corporation) was created in 1970 and since then major lines have pooled their resources, modernised and restored many of the fabulous trains of the past.

By Bus. Buses provide the most economical travel long distance, anywhere in the country, but they are also luxurious and efficient. Greyhound and Railways are the

Practical Information

two largest companies in the United States but there are at least one hundred others that cover about 100,00 miles. There are no sleeping facilities on buses but they are all air-conditioned, heated and most are equipped with washroom facilities, some even serve meals en route.

By Air. There are several international airlines, which fly directly and almost everyday of the week into LAX International Airport. Some overseas flights do, however, come via New York or San Francisco, but these can be checked with your travel agent or the airline direct.

> **INFOTIP:** Los Angeles International Airport is a potential panic-inducer. It is a sprawling complex, teeming with people and an apparently confusing layout for arrivals and departures. Actually this is a mirage as the airport functions quite efficiently once you take stock of your surroundings.

ELECTRICITY

The electric current in the United States is generally 110-115 volt, 60 cycle A.C. As this differs from most countries you must bring with you or buy on arrival an adapter for all electrical equipment such as electric razors, travel irons, hair dryers etc.

ENTERTAINMENT

Art Galleries

Los Angeles County Museum of Art 5905 Wilshire Blvd Tel.(213) 857 6222.
Tamara Bane 8025 Melrose Avenue Tel.(213) 651 1400.
Los Angeles Municipal Art Gallery 4804 Hollywood Blvd Tel.(213) 485 4581.

For more listings of gallleries, consult the:
Downtown Los Angeles Visitors Information Centre
695 S. Figueroa Street Los Angeles CA 90017
Tel.(213) 689 8822 or

Hollywood Visitors Information Centre The James House, James House Square, 6541 Hollywood Blvd Hollywood CA 90028 Tel. (213) 461 4231.

Practical Information

Children's Entertainment

Knott's Berry Farm 8039 Beach Blvd Buena Park CA 90620 Tel.(714) 220 5200.
Shake paws with Snoopy, pan for real gold, travel back 200 million years on the Kingdom of the Dinosours. Relive the exciting days of the Old West, thrill rides to a big time for little ones in picturesque Camp Snoopy.

Raging Waters 111 Raging Waters Drive San Dimas Tel (714) 592 6453/592 8181.
44 acres of slides, rides, chutes and lagoons. Take the kids to the Lil Dipper pool, or to any of the many rides for 'Lil Squirts'. Just bring your swimwear and suntan lotion.

Wild Rivers 8800 Irvine Centre Drive Laguna Hills CA 92653 Tel.(714) 768 WILD.
A wild time for everybody, from tiny tots to teenagers and adults. Rushing rivers, sheer-drop slides an fantastic surf, or relax at the soothing hot springs, lagoons and pint-sized pool.

Disneyland Walt Disney's aspiration to create a world in which the young at heart of all ages could laugh and play together has been fulfulled. a truly remarkable achievment, allow a full day.

Casinos and Card Clubs

The Bicycle Club Card Casino 7301 Eastern Avenue Bell Gardens CA 90201
Tel.(213) 806 4646.
Commerce Casino 6131 Telegraph Road Commerce CA 90040
Tel.(213) 721 2100.
Normandie Gambling Casino and Dinner Theatre 1045 W. Rosecrans Avenue
Gardena CA 91604 Tel.(213) 715 7428.

Cinema

More than three quarters of all movies in the United States are produced in the Los Angeles metropolitan area. Motion picture and television studios make their home here, movie buffs can discover all the secret and magic of the movie industry by visiting any one of the many studios located here.

Practical Information

Festivals and Public Holidays

Major annual events in and near Los Angeles:

January:
The Rose bowl Football Game on New Year's Day, played in Pasadena's Rose Bowl in Brookside Park.
Tournament of Roses Parade in Brookside Park.
Greater Los Angeles Auto show in the Convention Centre.

February:
Southern California Boat Show at the Los Angeles Convention Centre.
Open Golf Tournament in Pacific Palisades and the Winternationals
Championship Drag Races at Fairplex in Pomona.

April: Toyota Grand Prix at Long Beach.

May:
Home Show at the Los Angeles Convention Centre.
Renaissance Pleasure Faire in Agoura Hills.
UCLA's Mardi Gras and Arts and Crafts show in Westwood.

July:
On the 4th of July major fireworks displays at he Hollywood Bowl, the Rose Bowl and many other locations.
All-Star Shrine Football Game at eh Rose Bowl in Pasadena.
International Surf Festival, which rotates between Huntington Beach and Manhattan Beach.

August:
International Sea Festival at Long Beach.
Nisei Week in Little Tokyo and Sprots and Arts Festival in Santa Monica.

September:
Los Angeles County Fair in Pomona, on the largest in the United States.

October:
Ski Dazzle at the Los Angeles Convention Centre.

November:
Recreational Vehicles show at Dodger Stadium.

December:
Lighting of Christmas Tree Lane in Altadena, celebration at Disneyland and Las Posadas, Mexican Christmas Festival at El Pueblo de Los Angeles Historic Monument.

Practical Information

The Cross, Olvera Street

Public Holidays

News Year's Day	1 January
Martin Luther King Jnr's Birthday	3 January
Lincoln's Birthday	12 February
Washington's Birthday	3 February
Memorial Day	Last Monday in May
Labour Day	4 July
Admission Day	9 September
Columbus Day	2nd Monday in October
Veterans Day	11 November
Thanksgiving	23 November

Practical Information

Music/Orchestras/Concerts

The Greek Theatre 2700 N. Vermont Los Angeles CA 90027
Tel.(213) 410 1062.
The Groundling Theatre 7307 Melrose Avenue Los Angeles CA 90046
Tel.(213) 934 4747.
Los Angeles Pops 2425 Colorado Avenue Santa Monica CA 904043580
Tel.(213) 453 7677.
Los Angeles Chamber Orchestra 315 W. 9th StreetLos Angeles CA 90015
Tel.(213) 622 7001.
Los Angeles Philarmonica - Winter Season 135 N. Grand Avenue Los Angeles
CA 90012 Tel.(213) 972 7211.
Los Angeles Philarmonica - Summer Season 2301 N. Highland Avenue
Los Angeles CA 90078 Tel.(213) 850 2000.
Los Angeles Scottish Rite Cathederal & Auditorium 4357 Wilshire Blvd
Los Angeles CA 90010 Tel.(213) 937 1212.
The Pacific Theatre 100 Fair Drive Costa Mesa CA 92626
Tel.(213) 410 1062.
Universal Amphitheatre 100 Universal City Plaza Universal City CA 91608
Tel.(818) 980 9421.

Theatre

Ahmanson Theatre 135 N. Grand Avenue Los Angeles CA 90012
Tel.(213) 972 7403.
The Back Alley Theatre 15321 Burbank Blvd Van Nuys CA 91411
Tel.(818) 780 2240.
CCAL State L.A. Arts Complex 5154 State University Drive Los Angeles
CA 90032 Tel.(213) 224 2348.
Celebrity Theatre of Anaheim 201 E. Broadway Anahein CA 92805
Tel.(714) 535 2000.
Centre Theatre Group/Mark Taper Forum 135 N. Grand Avenue Los Angeles
CA 90012 Tel.(213) 972 7373.

Practical Information

Dorothy Chandler Pavilion 135 N. Grand Avenue Los Angeles CA 90012
Tel.(213) 972 7200.
The Henry Fonda Theatre 6162 Hollywood Blvd Los Angeles CA 90028
Tel.(213) 410 1062.
Los Angeles Theatre Centre 514 S. Spring Street Los Angeles CA 90013
Tel.(213) 627 5599.
Odyssey Theatre Ensemble 12111 Ohio Avenue Los Angeles CA 90025
Tel.(213) 826 1626.
The Pantages Theatre 6233 Hollywood Blvd Hollywood CA 90028
Tel.(213) 410 1062.
The Second City Theatre 214 Santa Monica Blvd Santa Monica CA 90401
Tel.(213) 451 0621.
The Shubert Theatre 2020 Avenue of the Stars Los Angeles CA 90067
Tel.(800) 233 3123.
Tamara 2035 N. Highland Avenue Los Angeles CA 90068
Tel.(213) 480 3232.
The Wilshire Theatre 8440 Wilshire Blvd Beverly Hills CA 90211   Tel.(213) 410 1062.

Olvera Street

Practical Information

Radio/Television

All major networks and many independent stations operate on both AM and FM radio. Several stations broadcast in Spanish and other languages as well as English. Major TV channels include 2(CBS), 4(NBC), 7(ABC) and 6 or 28(PBS).

Getting Around in Los Angeles

Buses:
Buslines provide comprehensive coverage of the entire metropolitan region. Route maps of the largest public transportation agency, RTD are available at the RTD Ticket Counter on Level B of the ARCO Plaza, 515 S. Flower Street, Tel 213-626-4455. A self guiding brochure outlines RTD routes and stops for nearly 100 tourist attractions in Southern California.

DASH (Downtown Area Short Hop) is a minibus shuttle system which operates at frequent intervals Monday to Saturday. The fare is 25c, exact change is required and it passes close to most business centres, retail stores, points of interest and major hotels in the central city.

Practical Information

Taxi:

Only taxis bearing the Los Angeles City Franchise seal are authorised to solicit fares in the downtown area. Fares are metered and are about $3.00 for the first mile and $1.60 for each additional mile. It is strongly recommended to phone for a taxi and always have a taxi telephone number with you, since very few taxis cruise outside areas of heavy tourist concentration.

The following is a selection of some companies:

Celebrity Red Top Tel 213-934-6700
Los Angeles Taxi Tel 213-747-5030
United Independent Tel 213-653-5050
Independent Tel 213-385-8294
Checker Tel 213-258-3231

> **INFOTIP:** The hotel bell boy can arrange for a limousine which costs not more than a taxi but is more comfortable. If you need a taxi or a limousine for a whole day, make arrangements direct with the driver, it will cost a lot less.

Catalina at night

Practical Information

San Gabriel Mission

Practical Information

Getting Outside of Los Angeles

By Rail:

Trailways share their main Los Angeles Terminal with Greyhound buses at the Greyhound/Trailways Transportation Centre 6th and Los Angeles Streets. The Passenger Terminal is at Los Angeles and Alameda Streets near the Civic Centre. Reservations and information are handled by **Amtrak**. Free Toll 800-872-7245.

By Sea:

Numerous steamship and cruise lines operate out of the city's manmade harbour, one of the largest ports in the United States. Admiral Cruises Inc. 140 W. 6th Street, San Pedro CA 90731, Tel 213-548-8411. 3-4 nights to Mexico, 7 day cruises to Mexico and Alaska. See also Tours and Cruises.

By Air:

Domestic Airlines:
Air Cal 575 W. Century Blvd Los Angeles CA 90045
Tel.(213) 627 5401.
Air Grand Canyon-Yosemite 3000 N. Clybourne Avenue Burbank
CA 91505, Tel.(818) 845-6074.
Air L.A. 3000 N. Clybourne Aveneu Burbank CA 91505
Tel.(213) 641 1114.
Alaska Airlines 6033 W. Century Blvd Los Angeles CA 90045
Tel.(800) 426-0333.
America West Airlines 10999 Riverside Drive North Hollywood
CA 91602, Tel.(818) 980 0150.
Southwest Airlines 5777 W. Century Blvd El Segundo CA 90045
Tel.(213) 670-3565.
US Air/Piedmont Airlines 6151 W. Century Blvd Los Angeles CA 90045, Tel.(213) 410 1732.

HELP

Questions regarding

Visa/Passports
Customs
Police
or in case of hospitalisation/death, your consulate should be notified.

Practical Information

Consulates

ARGENTINA CONSULATE GENERAL, Tel.(213) 739 9977

AUSTRALIAN CONSULATE GENERAL, Tel.(213) 380 0980

BAHAMAS TOURIST OFFICE Tel.(213) 385 0033

BEJING FESCO INTERNATIONAL, Tel.(213) 625 2750

BELGIAN CONSULATE GENERAL, Tel.(213) 385 8116

BELGIUM CONSULATE GENERAL, Tel.(213) 385 8116

BRITISH COLUMBIA CANADA, Government of, Tel.(213) 380 9171

BRITISH CONSULATE GENERAL, Tel.(213) 385 0252

CANADIAN CONSULATE GENERAL, Tel.(213) 687 7412

CONSULATE GENERAL OF PANAMA, Tel.(213) 627 9139

CONSULADO GENERAL DE MEXICO, Tel.(213) 624 3261

CONSULATE GENERAL DU CANADA, Tel.(213) 687 7432

CONSULATE GENERAL OF BOLIVIA, Tel.(213) 680 0190

CONSULATE GENERAL OF BRAZIL, Tel.(213) 382 3133

CONSULATE GENERAL OF LUXEMBOURG, Tel.(213) 394 2532

CONSULATE GENERAL OF SPAIN, Tel.(213) 658 6050

CONSULATE GENERAL OF CHILE, Tel.(213) 624 6357

CONSULATE GENERAL OF NETHERLANDS, Tel.(213) 380 3440

CONSULATE GENERAL OF GERMANY, Tel.(213) 930 2703

CONSULATE GENERAL OF JAPAN, Tel.(213) 624 8305

CONSULATE GENERAL OF PERU, Tel.(213) 975 1153

CONSULATE GENERAL OF SWITZERLAND, Tel.(213) 388 4127

Practical Information

CONSULATE GENERAL OF MALTA, Tel.(213) 685 6365

CONSULATE GENERAL OF JORDAN, Tel.(213) 216 4296

CONSULATE GENERAL OF NEW ZEALAND,
Tel.(213) 477 8241

FRENCH GOVERNMENT TOURIST OFFICE,
Tel.(213) 272 2661

GREEK NATIONAL TOURIST OFFICE, Tel.(213) 626 6695

If your country is not listed above consult the Yellow Pages telephone book or the hotel concierge.

Medical Emergencies

Police, Fire, Ambulance 911   When 911 answers, ask for Police, Fire or Ambulance. When the emergency service answers, be prepared to give the following information:
* Nature and exact locality of emergency
* If any persons are injured and if so how many?
* Your exact location.

Pharmacies
Day and night pharmacies are listed in the Yellow pages telephone book.

> **INFOTIP:** Remember medical, hospital and ambulance treatment are extremely expensive. Make sure you have adequate insurance before you leave home.

Police Emergencies

Dail 911

Death

The death of a foreign citizen requires instant notification of the relevant Consulate.
Other emergencies telephone numbers:

Coast Guard Long Beach, Tel.(213) 499 5555
Airport Police, Tel.(213) 646 4268
US Postal Inspection Service, Tel.(1) (800) 847 8847
California Missing Children Hotline, Tel.(1) (800) 222 3463
Rape Hotline, Tel.(213) 626 3393
Travellers Aid, Tel.(213) 686 0950

Practical Information

Lost Property

Advise the nearest police station immediately if the item is of significant value or if you can make a claim on your insurance. Bus companies, railways, taxis etc, have their own lost property office, so contact them first if this is where you left the item.

Replacement of certain items

Airline tickets - report the lost/theft to the airline and request replacement.

Credit cards/Traveller's cheques - report their loss or theft to the relevant company:

American Express Int Inc
Diners Card
Master Card
Thomas Cook
Visa Card

For other cards phone 411 telephone information.

Passport/drivers licence - in case of loss or theft advise your consulate immediatley.

Information for disabled people

Many thousands of attractions can be visited by disabled people. However, the wide range of attractions and the diversity of their physical characteristics make it difficult to note those that are completely accessible.

Practical Information

Please contact the Los Angeles Convention and Visitors Bureau at 695 S. Figueroa Street Los Angeles CA 90017 Tel.(213) 689 8822 in Dowtown L.A. or the Hollywood Visitor Information Centre, The James House Square, 6541 Hollywood Blvd, Hollywood Blvd Hollywood CA 90028 Tel.(213) 461 4213. Both are open between 9am-5pm Monday to Saturday.

For the deaf and hearing impaired. (TTY) call (800) 252 0940.

Crime

Unfortunately, theft and pickpocketing are common. If you are a victim, try to recall as much detail as possible. It is, however, rare for a stranger to be molested. If visiting the less respectable parts of Downtown L.A. it is unwise to dress like a flashy tourist and to wander around at night by yourself, as group of thieves operate at this time. If driving lock your car and leave any packages or **luggage** in the boot. It is also strongly recommended to leave jewellery in the hotels safe box.

Motoring

American Automobile Association (AAA) 2601 S. Figueroa Street
Los Angeles Tel.(213) 741 4070

Reciprocal services are available to members of recognised interstate and overseas Automobile Clubs. Bring your membership card with you. The AAA building is worth a visit plus you can obtain maps and travel information on the premises.

Traffic Laws

In America, vehicles drive on the right-hand side of the road. The speed limit on most streets is 35mph or as posted. Freeway speed is generally 55 mph.

Motorists may be ticketed for driving at speeds considered dangerously slow as will as dangerously fast. Right turns on red are allowed unless otherwise posted. The same applies for U-turns at Intersections. Pedestrians have always the right-of-way. The golden rule for driving the Los Angeles freeways is 'plan ahead'.

Parking

Although Downtown on street parking is prohibited in most areas during the day, Los Angeles has hundreds of

Practical Information

convenient parking lots or garages. Prices vary according to locations, and can be up to $2.00 per half hour or up to $12.00 per day. Most of the hotels however, and some stores, provide free parking.

In Case of Accident

Police will not attend minor accidents unless someone is injured. In case of more extensive damage and or injury call the emergency services on 911, tell the emergency operator that there is an injury or non injury accident. Let the emergency operator end the call. Do not hang up. Move the vehicle involved out of the traffic lanes, if it is disabled.

Rental Cars

The well-known national companies are represented in Los Angeles. In addition there is also a choice of local hire car operators. Rental charges may or may not include petrol, but usually allow unlimited miles. If you rent a car in one area and return it in another, there may be a repositioning fee.

To rent a car you must have a current driver's licence and must be over 16 years of age.

Some of the car hire firms in L.A.,

Ace Rent a Car, 6310 W. 89th Street, Los Angeles CA 90045
Tel.(213) 417 2220, Toll.(800) 223 3457
Alamo Rent a Car, 8900 Aviation Blvd, Inglewood CA 90301
Tel.(213) 649 2245
Avis Rent a Car, 360 N. Sepulveda Blvd, El Segundo CA 90245
Tel.(213) 615 4300
Budget Rent-a-Car, 9775 Airport Blvd, Los Angeles CA 90045
Tel.(213) 645 4500, Toll.(800) 527 0700
Budget Rent a Car - The Luxury Line, 300 S. La Cienega Blvd,
Los Angeles CA 90048, Tel.(213) 659 3473, Toll.(800) 826 7805
Budget Rent a Car - Luxury Line, 8747 Wilshire Blvd,
Beverly Hills CA 90211, Tel.(213) 657 1818, Toll.(800) 826 7805
Dollar Rent-a-Car Systmes, 6141 W. Century Blvd, Los Angeles CA 90045
Tel.(213) 776 8100, Toll.(800) 421 6868

Practical Information

Executive Rent a Car, 4900 W. Century Blvd, Inglewood CA 90304
Tel.(213) 674 3311, Toll.(800) 421 2424
Freedom Rent-a-Car, 8825B Sepulveda Blvd, Los Angeles CA 90045
Tel.(213) 645 3133, Toll.(800) 937 0999
The Hertz Corporation, 9000 Airport Blvd, Los Angeles CA 90045
Tel.(213) 646 4861, Toll.(800) 654 3131
Marathon Rent-a-Car, 5280 W. Century Blvd, Los Angeles CA 90045
Tel.(213) 645 2277, Toll.(800) 446 3737
Midway Rent-a-Car, 1601 S. Figueroa Street, Los Angeles CA 90015
Tel.(213) 749 4375
National Car Rental Systems Inc, 9419 Airport Blvd, Los Angeles
CA 90045 ,Tel.(213) 670 4950, Toll.(800) 227 7368
Southwest Car Rental, 12312 W. Olympic Blvd, West Los Angeles CA 90046
Tel.(213) 820 9393, Toll.(800) 824 8260
Thrifty Rent a Car of California Inc, 5440 W. Century Blvd, Los Angeles
CA 90045, Tel.(213) 645 1880, Toll.(800) 367 2277

Libraries

Los Angeles Central Libraries, 630 West 5th Street,
Tel.(213) 750 3573
Los Angeles County Law Library, 301 West 1st Street
Tel.(213) 629 3531
Theosophical Library Centre, 2416 N. Lake Avenue Alt
Tel.(818) 798 8020.

For other library branches consult the Yellow Pages telephone Book.

Post Office

Post office hours in the United States vary from 24 hours a day in central big city branches to 9am to 5pm in smaller cities and towns. On Saturdays the Post Office only open for half a day, if they open at all. Stamps can also be purchased in hotels, chemists, air and bus terminals etc.

Post Restante

In the United States it is called General Delivery.

Practical Information

This service is very helpful to visitors without, a fixed address. You simply have your mail addressed to your name, c/o General Delivery, at the main post office in the town that you are going to be in. You must, however, pick up, such mail personally, and, you must have suitable identification with you.

Religious Services

Church times: for times and venues, telephone numbers are listed below:
Anglican Church of Our Saviours & the Holy Apostles, Tel.935 0228
St Mary of the Angeles, Tel.660 2700
Apostolic Faith Church, Tel.759 4043
Armenian Catholic Church, Tel.261 9898
Bethel Assembly of God Church, Tel.(818) 956 3373
Community Baptist Church, Tel.636 7347
The Fundamentalist Baptist Tabernacle, Tel.380 9658
Community Bible Church, Tel.296 5379
Buddhist Vihara of L.A., Tel.464 9698
Good Shepherd, Beverly Hills, Tel.276 3139
Golden West Christian Church, Tel.413 1650
Central Church of Christ, Tel.389 1611
First Congregational Chruch of L.A., Tel.385 1341
All Saints Episcopal Parish of L.A., Tel.255 6806
Evangelica Church, Tel.731 4146
Greater Hebrew Missionary, Tel.759 0534
Masjid Bibal, Iban Rabah, Tel.291 0105
New Testament Cathedral, Tel.778 9935
Orthodox Church of Christ, Tel.258 3865
Bel-Vue Com. Uy. Presbyterian, Tel.757 9188

Other denominations are listed under Churches in the Yellow Pages telephone book.

It is expected that visitors will show respect for the Church both in dress and behaviour - this includes not taking photographs during the service.

Restaurants & Nightlife

Nightclubs

An evening on the town might find you at a poetry reading or catching a rising star at the comedy store. The city is a mecca for top-flight jazz, rock and country and western music.

Practical Information

THE ATRIUM LOUNGE, 555 Universal Terrace Parkway, Universal City
Los Angeles, Tel.(818) 506 2500

BOURBON STREET GROTTO, 350 S. Figueroa Street, Los Angeles CA 90071
Tel.(213) 629 4124.

CHIPPENDALES, 1024 S. Grand Avenue, Los Angeles CA90071
Tel.(213) 396 4045

CINEGRILL, 7000 Hollywood Blvd, Hollywood CA 90028
Tel.(213) 466 7000

THE COMEDY STORE, 8433 Sunset Blvd, West Hollywood CA 90069
Tel.(213) 656 6225

FANTASIA, THE NIGHTCLUB OF TOMORROW, 4th and S. Flower Streets
Los Angeles, CA 90071, Tel.(213) 623 2623

GALLERY BAR, 506 S. Grand Avenue, Los Angeles CA 90071
Tel.(213) 624 1011

GRAND AVENUE BAR, 506 S. Grand Avenue, Los Angeles CA 90071
Tel.(213) 624 1011

HOLLYWOOD LIVE, INC, 6840 Hollywood Blvd, Hollywood CA 90028
Tel.(213) 461 6222

IMPROVISION, 8162 Melrose Avenue, Los Angeles CA 90046
Tel.(213) 651 2583

INDIGO JAZZ CLUB, 111 E. Artesia Blvd, Compton CA 90221
Tel.(213) 632 1234

LA CAGE AUX FOLLIES, 643 N. La Cienaga Blvd, West Hollywood CA 90069
Tel.(213) 657 1091

LAUGH FACTORY, 8001 Sunset Blvd, Los Angeles CA 90046
Tel.(213) 656 1336

Practical Information

PROMENADE, 123 S. Lincoln Avenue, Monterey Park CA 91754
Tel.(818) 571 8818

SAUSALITO SOUTH, 3280 Sepulveda Blvd, Manhattan Beach CA 90266
Tel.(213) 546 4507

SIR WINSTON'S PIANO BAR, Pier J, Long Beach CA 90801
Tel.(213) 435 3511

STEFANINO'S FINE SEAFOOD RESTAURANT & DISCO, 9229 Sunset Blvd
Los Angeles CA 90069, Tel.(213) 550 1544

VERTIGO, 333 Boylston Street, Los Angeles CA 90017
Tel.(213) 481 0273

Fireworks at Hollywood Bowl

Practical Information

Restaurants

Dining may be a serious business in Los Angeles, but that doesn't mena that it has to be expensive or formal. New restaurants achieve overnight success, only to give way quickly to the next trend. The city that was once considered a wasteland now rivals the world's great food capitals. Los Angeles has so many restaurants that it would be possible to eat at a different one every night for a year, and still not visit them all. Here is a selection.

Downtown Los Angeles

ANGEL'S FLIGHT, 711 S. Hope Street, Los Angeles CA 90017
Tel.(213) 683 1234.

BOURBON STREET GROTTO, 350 S. Figueroa Street, Los Angeles CA 90071
Tel.(213) 629 4124.

CAFETERIA IN THE COURT AT WELLS FARGO CENTRE, 330 S. Hope Street
Los Angeles CA 90071 Tel.(213) 617 7072.

CARDINI, 930 Wilshire Blvd, Los Angeles CA 90017
Tel.(213) 629 4321.

CITY GRILL, LOS ANGELES HILTON HOTEL, 930 Wilshire Blvd,
Los Angeles CA 90017, Tel.(213) 629 4321.

EL CHOLO, 1121 S. Western Avenue, Los Angeles CA 90006
Tel.(213) 734 2773.

EL PASEO DE LOS ANGELES RESTAURANT, E-11 Olvera Street,
Los Angeles CA 90012, Tel.(213) 626 1361.

ENGINE CO. NO 28 RESTAURANT, 644 S. Figueroa Street
Los Angeles CA 90017, Tel.(213) 624 6996.

GARDEN RESTAURANT AT LAWRY'S CALIFORNIA CENTRE, 570 W. Avenue 26
Los Angeles CA 90065, Tel.(213) 224 6850.

GILL'S CUISINE OF INDIA, 838 S. Grand Avenue, Los Angeles CA 90017
Tel.(213) 623 1050, Toll.(800) 553 4774.

Practical Information

HONG KONG LOW RESTAURANT, 425 Ginling Avenue, Los Angeles CA 90012
Tel.(213) 628 6217.

ITALIAN KITCHEN, 420 W. 8th Street, Los Angeles CA 90014
Tel.(213) 622 9277.

LA GOLONDRINA CAFE, W-17 Olvera Street, Los Angeles CA 90012
Tel.(213) 628 4349.

LAS ANITAS' RESTAURANT, W-26 Olvera Street, Los Angeles CA 90012
Tel.(213) 623 2883.

LAS FRERES TAIX RESTAURANT, 1911 Sunset Blvd, Los Angeles CA 90026
Tel.(213) 484 1265.

THE ORIGINAL SONORA CAFE, 445 S. Figueroa Street, Los Angeles
CA 90071, Tel.(213) 624 1800.

PACIFIC DINING CAR, 1310 W. 6th Street, Los Angeles CA 90017
Tel.(213) 483 6000.

PAVILION RESTAURANT, 165 N. Grand Avenue, Los Angeles CA 90012
Tel.(213) 972 7333.

THE STOCK EXCHANGE, 618 S. Spring Street, Los Angeles CA 90014
Tel.(213) 627 4467.

TAMAYO RESTAURANT, 5300 E. Olympic Blvd, Los Angeles CA 90022
Tel.(213) 260 4700.

Hollywood

ANNA MARIA RISTORANTE ITALIANO, 1356 S. La Brea, Los Angeles CA 90019
Tel.(213) 935 2089.

BUTTERFIELD'S RESTAURANT, 8426 Sunset Blvd, West Hollywood CA 91604
Tel.(213) 656 3055.

Practical Information

CHIANTI/CHIANTI CUCINA, 7383 Melrose Avenue, Los Angeles CA 90046
Tel.(213) 653 8333.

DAR MAGHREB RESTAURANT, 7651 Sunset Blvd, Los Angeles CA 90046
Tel.(213) 876 7651.

HUGO'S RESTAURANT, 8401 Santa Monica Blvd, West Hollywood CA 90069
Tel.(213) 654 3993.

KINGSLEY GARDEN VEGETARIAN RESTAURANT, 4070 W. Third Street
Los Angeles CA 90020 Tel.(213) 487 1780.

LA MASIA, 9077 Santa Monica Blvd, West Hollywood CA 90069
Tel.(213) 273 7066.

LA VILLA TAXCO, 7038 Sunset Blvd, Los Angeles CA 90028
Tel.(213) 469 5131.

TAM O'SHANTER INN, 2980 Los Feliz Blvd, Los Angeles CA 90039
Tel.(213) 664 0228

TOM BERGIN'S, 840 S. Fairfax Avenue, Los Angeles CA 90036
Tel.(213) 936 7151.

TONY ROMA'S, A PLACE FOR RIBS, 666 Universal Terrace Parkway,
Universal City CA 916081802, Tel.(818) 777 3939.

YAMASHIRO, 1999 N. Sycamore, Hollywood CA 90068
Tel.(213) 466 5125.

Westside

AT MARTY'S, 8657 W. Pico Blvd, Los Angeles CA 90035
Tel.(213) 272 1048.

BENIHANA, 38 N. La Cienega Blvd, Beverly Hills CA 90211
Tel.(213) 655 7311.

BOMBAY PALACE, 8690 Wilshire Blvd, Beverly Hills CA 90211
Tel.(213) 659 9944.

Practical Information

COLETTE, 9360 Wilshire Blvd, Beverly Hills CA 90212
Tel.(213) 273 1400, Toll.(800) 421 0545.

GINGER MAN RESTAURANT - CARROLL O'CONNOR'S PLACE, 369 N. Bedford Drive
Beverly Hills CA 90210, Tel.(213) 273 7585

HARD ROCK CAFE, 8600 Beverly Hills, Los Angeles CA 90048
Tel.(213) 276 7605.

JIMMY'S, 201 Moreno Drive, Beverly Hills CA 90212
Tel.(213) 879 2394.

LA SCALA RESTAURANT, 9455 Santa Monica Blvd, Beverly Hills CA 90210
Tel.(213) 275 0579.

R.J.'S THE RIB JOINT, 252 N. Beverly Drive, Beverly Hills CA 90210
Tel.(213) 274 7427.

RANGOON RACQUET CLUB, 9474 Santa Monica Blvd, Beverly Hills CA 90210
Tel.(213) 274 8926.

Hollywood and Bowl

Practical Information

Santa Monica and Malibu

ACAPULCO MEXICAN RESTAURANT, SANTA MONICA, 3360 Ocean Park Bvld
Santa Monica CA 90405, Tel.(213) 450 8665.

CITY OF ANGELS BREWING COMPANY, 1445 Fourth Street, Santa Monica
CA 90401, Tel.(213) 451 0096.

THE FISH COMPANY SANTA MONICA, 174 Kinney Street, Santa Monica
CA 90405, Tel.(213) 392 8366.

MALIBU SEA LION U.S.A, 21150 Pacific Coast Highway, Malibu CA 90265
Tel.(213) 456 2810.

1000 WILSHIRE RESTAURANT, 1000 Wilshire Blvd, Santa Monica CA 90404, Tel.(213) 395 1000.

VERDI RISTORANTE DI MUSICA, 1519 Wilshire Blvd, Santa Monica CA 90403
Tel.(213) 393 0706.

Practical Information

Marina Del Rey, Venice

CASA ESCOBAR, 14160 Palawan Way, Marina del Rey CA 90292
Tel.(213) 822 2199.

EDIE'S DINER, 4211 Admiralty Way, Marina del Rey CA 90292
Tel.(213) 823 5339.

REUBEN'S STEAKHOUSE & FRENCH SEAFOOD, 4211 Admiralty Way
Marina del Rey CA 90292.

SHANGHAI RED'S RESTAURANT, 13813 Fiji Way, Marina del Rey CA 90291
Tel.(213) 823 4522.

THE WAREHOUSE RESTAURANT, 4499 Admiralty Way, Marina del Rey CA 90292
Tel.(213) 823 5451.

Airport Area

ACAPULCO MEXICAN RESTAURANT, PLAYA DEL REY, 8360 W. Manchester Blvd
Playa del Rey CA 90293, Tel.(213) 822 4031.

BARNABEY'S RESTAURANT & PUB, 3501 Sepulveda Blvd, Manhattan Beach
CA 90266, Tel.(213) 545 8466, Toll.(800) 421 0341.

SAUSALITO SOUTH, 3280 Sepulveda Blvd, Manhattan Beach CA 90266
Tel.(213) 546 4507.

South Bay and Beach Cities

ALPINE INN AT ALPINE VILLAGE, 833 W. Torrance Blvd, Torrance CA 90503
Tel.(213) 327 4384.

BABOUCH MOROCCAN RESTAURANT, 810 S. Gaffey Street, San Pedro CA 90731
Tel.(213) 831 0246.

CASA MARIA, 3301 Atlantic Avenue, Long Beach CA 90807
Tel.(213) 595 1795.

Practical Information

CHELSEA (HOTEL QUEEN MARY), Pier J, Long Beach CA 90801
Tel.(213) 435 3511.

SHERATON AT REDONDO BEACH RESTAURANT, 300 N Harbor Drive
Redondo Beach CA 902772552, Tel.(213) 318 8888.

Daytime Concert

Practical Information

The Valleys

THE CASTAWAY, 1250 E. Harvard Road, Burbank CA 91501
Tel.(818) 848 6691.

CHARLEY BROWN'S, 20401 Ventura Blvd, Woodland Hills CA 91364
Tel.(818) 348 1812.

MY WAY RESTAURANT, 6304 Laurel Canyon Blvd, North Hollywood
CA 91606, Tel.(818) 761 5490.

SWISS PARK RESTAURANT, 1905 Workman Mill Road, Whittier CA 90601
Tel.(213) 699 1525.

BENIHANAH, 4250 Birch Street, Newport Beach CA 92660
Tel.(714) 955 0822.

BOB BURNS RESTAURANT, 37 Fashion Island, Newport Beach CA 92660
Tel.(714) 644 2030.

KNOTT'S BERRY FARM CHICKEN DINNER RESTAURANT, 8039 Beach Blvd,
Buena Park CA 90620, Tel.(714) 220 5080.

KNOTT'S BERRY FARM'S FAMILY STEAK HOUSE, 8039 Beach Blvd
Buena Park CA 90620, Tel.(714) 827 1776.

Dinner Theatres

EL CID SHOW RESTAURANT, 4212 W. Sunset Blvd, Hollywood CA 90029 Tel.(213) 668 0318.

HARLEQUIN DINNER PLAYHOUSE, 3503 S. Harbor Blvd, Santa Ana CA 92704 Tel.(714) 979 5511.

MEDIEVAL TIMES, 7662 Beach Blvd, Buena Park CA 90622
Tel.(714) 521 4740, Toll.(800) 826 5358.

NORMANDI GAMBLING CASINO AND DINNER THEATRE, 1045 W. Rosecrans Avenue
Gardena CA 91604, Tel.(213) 715 7428.

Practical Information

Shopping

No trip to L.A. is complete without at least one visit to a department store. Here, trends are born and fashions originate, boutiques, department stores and unique shops reflect tastes and styles as diverse as the consumers who frequent them. With gigantic shopping malls that stretch for mile, L.A. is the nation's number one retail market.

Shopping Plazas and Malls

ATLANTIC RICHFIELD PLAZA, 505 S. Flower Street, Level C
Los Angeles CA 90071, Tel.(213) 625 2132.
BEVERLY CENTRE, 8500 Beverly Blvd, Los Angeles CA 90048
Tel.(213) 854 0070.
BONAVENTURE SHOPPING GALLERY, 404 S. Figueroa Street
Los Angeles CA 90071, Tel.(213) 687 0680.
BROADWAY PLAZA, 750 W. Seventh Street, Los Angeles CA 90017
Tel.(213) 624 2891.
CENTURY CITY SHOPPING CENTRE, 10250 Santa Monica Blvd
Los Angeles CA 90067, Tel.(213) 553 5300.
THE COOPER BUILDING, 860 S. Los Angeles Street, Los Angeles CA 90014
Tel.(213) 622 1139.
FARMERS MARKET AND SHOPPING VILLAGE, 6333 W. 3rd Street
Los Angeles CA 90036, Tel.(213) 933 9211.
FOX HILLS MALL, 200 Fox Hills Mall, Culver City CA 90230
Tel.(213) 390 7833.
GLENDA GALLERIA, 2148 Glendale Galleria, Glendale CA 91210
Tel.(818) 240 9536.
JAPANESE VILLAGE PLAZA, 327 E. 2nd Street, Los Angeles CA 90012
Tel.(213) 620 8861.
SANTA MONICA PLAZA, 2nd & 4th Street, Colorado & Broadway
Santa Monica CA 90401, Tel.(213) 394 5451.
SEVENTH MARKET PLACE AT CITICORP PLAZA, 735 S. Figueroa Street
Los Angeles CA 90017, Tel.(213) 955 7170.
SHERMAN OAKS FASHION SQUARE, 13760 Riverside Drive
Sherman Oaks CA 91423 Tel.(818) 783 0550.

Practical Information

WESTSIDE PAVILLION, 10800 W. Picco Blvd, West Los Angeles CA 90064
Tel.(213) 450 1757.

Department and Speciality Stores

GUMPS, 9560 Wilshire Blvd, Beverly Hills CA 90212
Tel.(213) 278 3200.

I MAGNIN & CO, 9634 Wilshire Blvd, Beverly Hills CA 90212
Tel.(213) 271 2131.

J.W ROBINSON COMPANY, 9900 Wilshire Blvd, Beverly Hills CA 90210
Tel. (213) 275 5464.

NEIMAN-MARCUS, 9700 Wilshire Blvd, Beverly Hills CA 90212
Tel.(213) 550 5900.

SAKS FIFTH AVENUE, 9600 Wilshire Blvd, Beverly Hills CA 90212
Tel.(213) 275 4211.

Shopping Complex

THE BEVERLY CENTRE, 8500 Beverly Blvd, Los Angeles CA 90048
Tel.(213) 854 9700.

RODEO COLLECTION LTD, 421 N. Rodeo Drive, Beverly Hills CA 90210
Tel.(213) 275 9700.

Duty Free Shops

DUTY FREE SHOPPERS WEST, 5730 Arbor Vitae, Los Angeles CA 90045
Tel.(213) 642 1972.

DUTY FREE SHOPPERS WEST, 637 Wilshire Blvd, Los Angeles CA 90009
Tel.(213) 628 0375.

Rodeo Drive

At the top of the shopping list is Rodeo Drive. Not more than two blocks long, Rodeo is as good if not better than Madison Avenue in New York, Bond Street in London, and

Practical Information

the Rue du Faubourg, Saint Honore in Paris. If your interests are cultural, be sure to visit the small complex on the west side of the street designed by architect Frank Lloyd Wright. It's a maze of small shops tucked away on several levels. The ultra-expensive, chic interior design shops try to lure customers with such gimmicks as complimentary drinks, free shoe shines and a degree of pampering not found anywhere else. The Beverly Hills Chamber of Commerce offers personal shopping escorts or 'ambassadors' to help visitors through the numerous shopping choices.

Listed below are just some of the most fabulous places in Rodeo Drive, Beverly Hills:

Alfred Dunhil, No 201, Tel.(213) 274 5351
Fred Hayman, No 273, Tel.(213) 271 3000
Chanel Inc., No 301, Tel.(213) 278 5500
Hammacher Schelemmer, No 309, Tel.(213) 859 7255
Adrienne Vittadini, No 319, Tel.(213) 275 9841
Hermes, No 343, Tel.(213) 278 6440
Gucci, No 347, Tel.(213) 278 3451
Mr Guy, No 369, Tel.(213) 275 4143
Fred Joaillier Inc, No 401, Tel.(213) 278 3733
Vidal Sasson, No 405, Tel.(213) 274 8791
Nina Ricci, No 431, Tel.(213) 858 8081
Theodore Man, No 451, Tel.(213) 274 8029
Theodore, No 453, Tel.(213) 276 9691
Lina Lee, No 459, Tel.(213) 556 2678
Claude Montana, No 469, Tel.(213) 273 7925
Kent and Curwen, No 474, Tel.(213) 274 0233
Carroll and Co, No 466, Tel.(213) 274 7319
Bigi, No 458, Tel.(213) 276 3537
Polo/Ralph Laurens, No 444, Tel.(213) 281 7200
Giorgio Armani, No 436, Tel.(213) 271 5555
Elizabeth Arden, No 434, Tel.(213) 273 9980
Valentino, No 414, Tel.(213) 271 5150
Maud Frizon, No 414, Tel.(213) 271 5150
Cartier, No 370, Tel.(213) 275 4272
Cecil Gee, No 346, Tel.(213) 858 8857
Christie's, No 342, Tel.(213) 275 5334
Bally, No 340, Tel.(213) 271 0666
Diamond on Rodeo, No 332, Tel.(213) 278 2811
Jax, No 324, Tel.(213) 276 5761
David Orgell, No 320, Tel.(213) 272 3355
Battaglia, No 306, Tel.(213) 276 7184
Van Cleef & Arpels, No 300, Tel.(213) 276 1161

Shopping Hours

Hours are usually 9 or 10am to 7 or 8pm, a lot of shops are open seven day a week.

Practical Information

Sports and Athletics

Los Angeles is the sports centre of the nation. Two professional baseball teams, two professional basketball teams, two professional football teams, professional hockey, rodeo, polo and numerous other sport clubs compete for a share of the action.

Southern California is the home of some of the best private golf courses, in the world, but there is no shortage of public courses.

Sporting Complexes

LOS ANGELES MEMORIAL COLISUM, 3911 S. Figueroa, Los Angeles
Tel.(213) 748 6131.

THE FORUM, 3900 Manchester & Prairie Blvd, Inglewood
Tel.(213) 674 6000.

SPORTS ARENA, 3939 S. Figueroa, Los Angeles Tel.(213) 748 6131.

DODGER STADIUM, 1000 Elysian Park Avenue, Los Angeles
Tel.(213) 224 1400.

HOLLYWOOD PARK RACE TRACK, 1050 S. Prairie Blvd, Inglewood
Tel.(213) 677 7151.

SANTA ANITA THOROUGHBRED RACING, 285 W. Huntington Drive
Arcadia, Tel.(213) 444 2171.

PAULEY PAVILION, UCLA, UCLA Campus, Westwood Blvd, Westwood
Tel.(213) 825 2101.

BASEBALL L.A. Dodgers and California Angeles open baseball season April to August.

For tickets L.A. Dodgers Tel.(213) 224 1500.
For tickets Cal. Angeles Tel.(714) 634 2000.

BASKETBALL Los Angeles Lakers contact The Forum Tel.(213) 674 6000 Los Angeles Clippers contact, Sports Arena Tel.(213) 748 6131
HORSEBACK RIDING Griffith Park, 4730 Crystal Springs Road, Tel. 665 5188.

Practical Information

Coliseum and Sports Arena

Anaheim Stadium

Practical Information

POLO Call the Los Angeles Equestrial Centre as it is played at Indio, Santa Barbara and Los Angeles on a regular basis, Tel.(1)(800) 840 9066.

SPORTFISHING Charters are available from Redondo Beach, Marina Del Rey, Long Beach, San Pedro and Malibu.

THROUGHBRED RACING At Hollywood Park the season begins in April. Inglewood Tel. 419 1500.

At Santa Anita the season begins in October Tel.(1)(800) 574 7223.

QUARTER-HORSE RACING Los Alanitos, Long Beach throughout the year.

TENNIS COURTS, PUBLIC

Beverly Hills High School, 241 Moreno Drive, Beverly Hills
Tel.(213) 277 5900.

La Cienega Park Tennis Courts, 8400 Gregony Way, Beverly Hills
Tel.(213) 550 4767.

Rancho Park, Cheviot Hills Tennis, 2551 Motor Avenue, Los Angeles
Tel.(213) 836 8879.

Roxbury Park Tennis Courts, 471 S. Moreno Drive, Beverly Hills
Tel.(213) 550 4979.

Ritz-Carlton, Laguna Niguel, Laguna Niguel Tel.(714) 240 2000.

GOLF COURSES, PUBLIC

Rancho Park Golf Course, 10460 W. Pico Blvd, Los Angeles
Tel.(213) 838 7373.

Griffith Park, 4730 Crystal Springs Drive, Los Angeles
Tel.(213) 663 2555.

Ritz-Carlton, Laguna Niguel, 33533 Ritz-Carlton Drive, Laguna Niguel
Tel.(714) 240 2000.

Practical Information

Parks with Sports Facilities

COLDWATER CANYON PARK, 1100 Coldwater Canyon Drive
Facilities: putting green, jogging track.

LA CIENEGA PARK, 8400 Gregory Way
Facilities: tennis courts, basketball courts, two baseball diamonds, soccer fields, putting green.

ROXBURG PARK, 471 S. Roxburg Drive
Facilities: tennis courts, basketball courts, putting green, lawnbowling, soccer fields, baseball field.

WATER RECREATION, Mainly at Big Bear, Lake Arrowhead and Lake Casita, but numerous reservoirs include waterskiing and sailing.

Sailing lessons are available at Marina del Rey, Long Beach and San Pedro.

> **INFOTIP:** The city is blessed with some excellent parks. However it is wise for visitors to stick to the populated areas and main paths. Don't wander off into secluded corners.

The Rose Bowl

Practical Information

Telephones and Telegrams

Public telephones can be found everywhere, in transportation terminals, chemists, hotel lobbies, restaurants, pavement kiosks and even along highways.

Telephone directories are found beside almost every phone, except those in exterior locations. There are two types of directories, the White Pages (General) with alphabetical surnames listings and the Classified (Yellow pages) with business and services in alphabetical order. Local calls cost from 10c to 20c each. To make a long distance call dial '0' for the operator and make sure that you have plenty of coins in particular 25c coins, or you can use your American Express or Visa Card for a credit card call.

You can send a domestic telegram or an overseas cablegram from the hotel or simply go to the nearest Western Union, an organization which specializes in telegraphic communications world wide.

Public Telephones

Local calls can be made from public telephone booths or from your hotel room.

Long Distance and Overseas Calls

International Direct Distance Dialling is available from most telephones in California, by using either a major credit card or coins.

Dial the International Access Code 011, plus country code plus city code, plus telephone number.

For additional assistance or information dial '00' (operator).

Codes for all American cities and most country codes can be found in the white pages. Calls to the Bahamas, Bermuda, Canada, Puerto Rico and the Virgin Islands can be dialed in the same manner as long distance calls within the United States.

Tipping

Tipping is not compulsory and is not automatically included into the bill or fare. Waiters and taxi drivers are customarilly awarded 15 percent of the bill or fare increasing to 20 percent for excellent service. Bartenders, doormen, bellhops or skycaps usually get $0.57 - $0.75 per drink or bag carried.

Practical Information

Time

To determine the time in the countries listed below, add the hours shown under PST. Or if the hours are proceded by a minus sign, subtract from your time.

Australia	18	Germany	9
Austria	9	Greece	10
Belguim	9	Hong Kong	16
Brazil	5	Singapore	16
Cyprus	10	Spain	9
France	9	United Kingdom	8

TOURS AND CRUISES

Cruises

Admiral Cruises, Inc., 140 W. 6th Street, San Pedro, Tel.(213) 548 8411.

3-4 nights cruises to Mexico, and
7 nights crises to Mexico and Alaska.

BLUE WATER ADVENTURES/CHARTER CONCEPTS, 13757 Fiji Way
Marina del Rey Tel.(213) 301 8089.
Catalina Island, daysails, sportfishing, dinner/dance and Harbour cruises.
CATALINA CHANNEL EXPRESS, Berth 95, P.O. Box 1391
San Pedro CA 90733 Tel.(213) 519 1212.
Fast, comfortable, airline style 90 min ride to Catalina.
FANTASEA CHARTERS, 1888 Century Park East, Los Angeles
Tel.(213) 556 2628.
Private and corporate yacht charte, with licensed Bar and catering staff.
MARINA CRUSE LINE, 13727 Fiji Way, Marina del Rey
Tel.(213) 301 6000.
Harbour cruise, the bill includes fare and entertainment.
SPIRIT OF LOS ANGELES, Tel.(213) 514 2999.
Lunch, dinner or a moonlight cruise in the Port of Los Angeles.

Tours

ALEXAIR HELICOPTERS TOURS, Ports O'Call Village, Berth 75
San Pedro Tel.(213) 519 1523.

Practical Information

JET HELICOPTERS TOURS, L.A. Nighthawks, Beverly Hills
Tel. (213) 859 1171.
JAZZ COMEDY, ROCK NIGHTCLUBS, Nippon Trovel, 611 W. Sixth Street
Los Angeles, Tel.(213) 627 2820.

Sightseeing for Individuals and Groups

STARLINE SIGHTSEEING TOURS, 6845 Hollywood Blvd, Hollywood
Tel.(213) 463 3131.
TIFFANY TOURS, Tel.(213) 642 0555.
AGENTOURS INC., Tel.(213) 473 2456.
AIR L.A., Tel.(213) 641 1114.
CALIFORNIA WINE TOURS, Tel.(213) 302 1475.

TOURIST SERVICES

The Los Angeles Convention and Visitors bureau invite all to stop at the following Visitor Information Centres:

DOWNTOWN L.A., 695 South Figueroa Street, Los Angeles
Tel.(213) 689 8822.

HOLLYWOOD, 6541 Hollywood Blvd, James House Square
Tel.(213) 461 4213.

AUTOMOBILE CLUB OF SOUTHERN CALIFORNIA, 2601 South Figueroa Street
Los Angeles Tel.(213) 741 3111.

TRAVELLER'S AID, 24 Hour Infoline, Tel.(213)686 0950.

THE METRIC SYSTEM

Area

1 hectare 10000m/sqr or 2.47 acres

Converting hectares to acres, multiply the number of hectares by 2.47 (e.g. 10 ha x 2.47 24.7 acres)
Converting acres to hectares, multiply the number of acres by .41 (e.g. 40 acres x .41 16.4 ha)

Practical Information

Capacity

1 litre   33.92 ounces
            1.06 quart
0.26 gallons

Converting litres to gallons, multiply the number of litres by .26. (e.g. 20l x .26 5.2 gallons)
Converting gallons to litres multiply number of gallons by 3.79. (e.g. 10 gal x 3.79 37.9l)

Weight

1 gram 0.04 ounces
1 kilogram 2.2 pounds

Converting kilograms to pounds, multiply number of kilos by 2.2. (e.g. 55 kg x 2.2 121 pounds)
Converting pounds to kilograms, multiply number of pounds by .45. (e.g. 100 pounds x .45 45 kilos)

Length

1 millimetre   0.04 inches
1 centimetre   0.39 inches
1 metre   1.09 yards
1 kilometre   0.62 mile

Converting kilometres to miles is as simple as multiplying the number of kilometres by 0.62.(e.g. 10km's x 0.62 6.2 miles)
Converting miles to kilometres is done by multyplying the number of miles by 1.61 (e.g. 60mi x 1.61 96.6km's)

Temperature

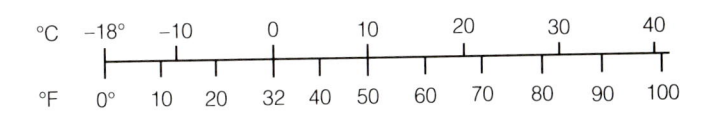

°C -18° -10   0   10   20   30   40
°F   0° 10 20 32 40 50 60 70 80 90 100

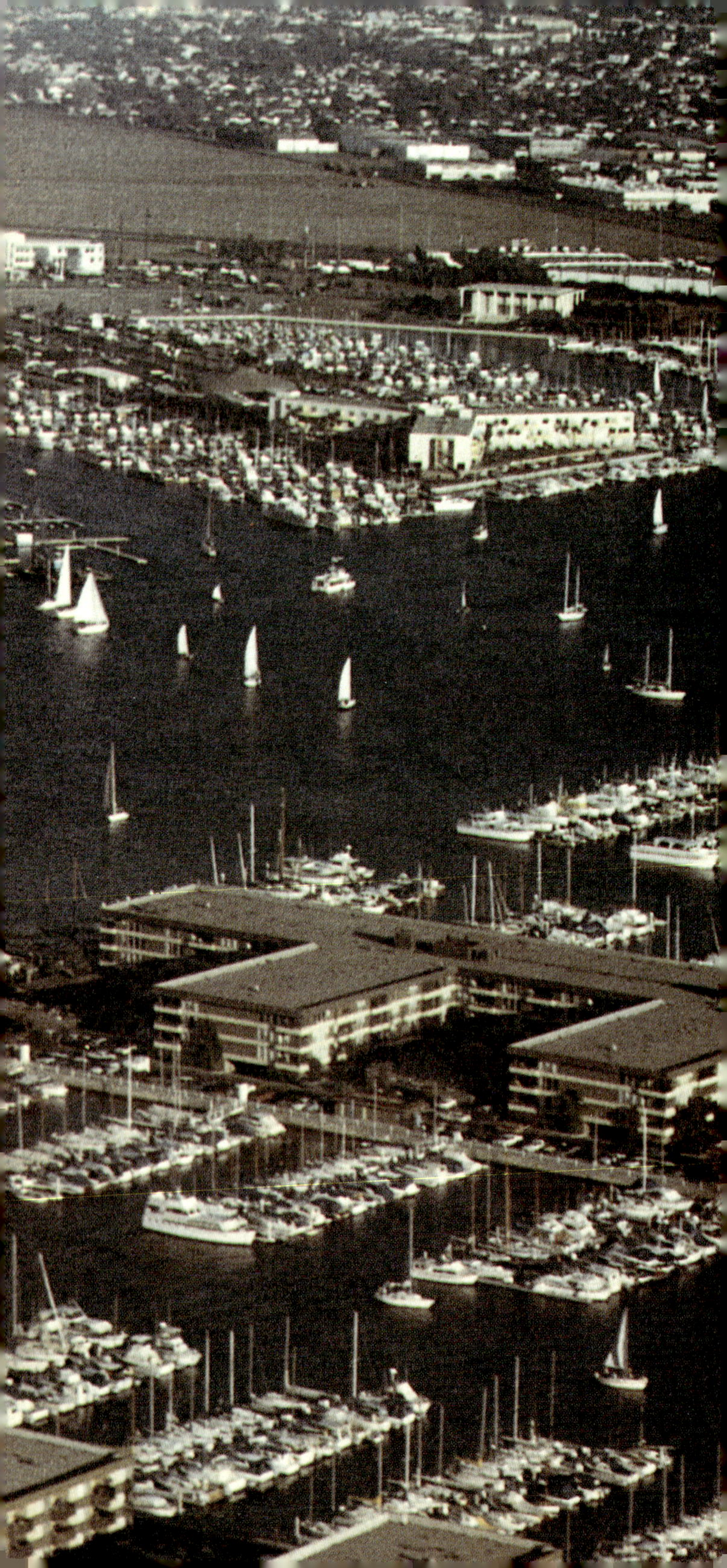

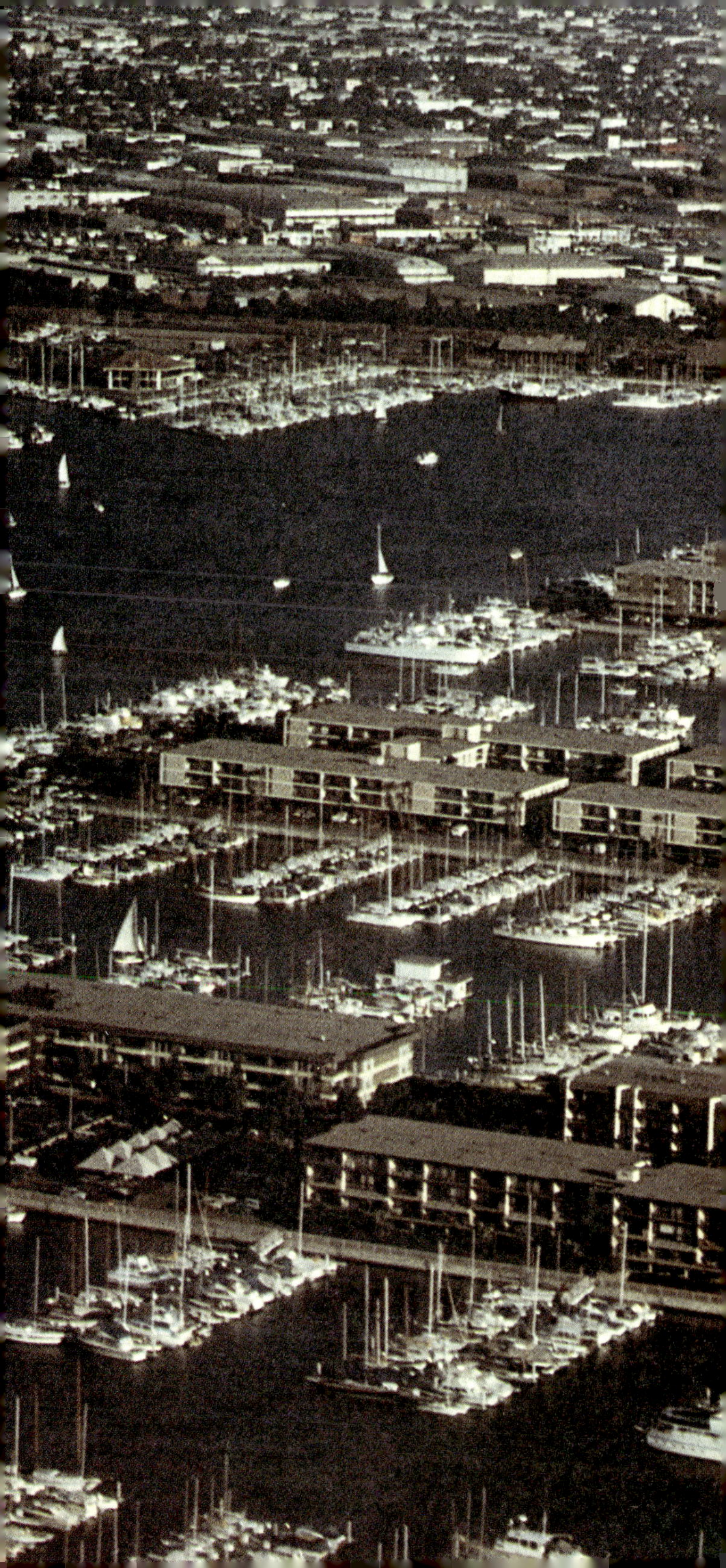

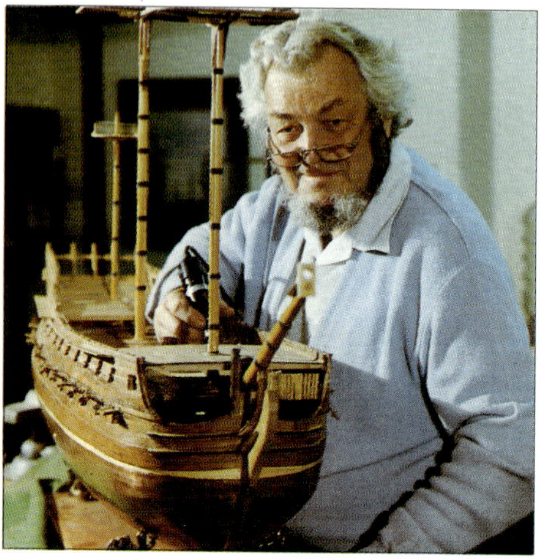

PART V
Business Guide

Samuel Cunard

BUSINESS GUIDE

Contents

Banks
Business Briefing
Business Publications
Chamber of Commerce
Convention Facilities
Credit Cards
Exchange, Import/Export of Currency
General Notes
Major Airlines

Home to 3.4 million people, Los Angeles is more than just a city, it is the centre of a thousand different industries, activities and the business hub of the nation.

Growth, economic prosperity and international trade have transformed Los Angeles into the country's leading financial and business centre.

Being the gateway to the Pacific rim, Los Angeles plays a major role in international trade.

In fact, if Los Angeles were a country, its gross national product would be 6th in the world.

Business Briefing

Major Industries: There are seven basic industries in Los Angeles area with employment shares varying between 6 and 9 per cent, and more than 450,000 workers. Business, Professional and Finance (Banking, Savings and Loans), Engineering Services, Computer programmes Aerospace Tourism.

Major exports: include machinery and equipment, electrical equipment, aerospace equipment, instruments and refined petroleum products.

Major imports: include electrical machinery and equipment, motor vehicles, machinery, oil and apparel.

Principal trading partners: Japan, South Korea, Hong Kong, Taiwan, West Germany, Australia, United Kingdom, Canada and Mexico.

Import/Export of Currency

U.S. currency can be taken out of the country up to $10,000.00.

Any amount in excess of $10,000.00 must be accompanied by a and U.S. Customs declaration.

Business Guide

Banks

El Camino Bank, 100 N Harbor Blvd, Anaheim CA 92805, Tel. (714) 491 3100, Fax. (714) 491 3107.

City National Bank, 400 N Roxbury Drive, Beverly Hills CA 90210, Tel. (213) 550 5400, Fax. (213) 274 9567.

American International Bank, 624 S. Grand Ave, Los Angeles CA 90017, Tel. (213) 688 8600,
Fax. (213) 688 8680.

California Commerce Bank, 615 Flower Street, 12th Floor, Los Angeles CA 90017, Tel. (213) 624 5700,
Fax. (213) 488 2685.

California Korea Bank, 1133 Wilshire Blvd, Los Angeles CA 90017, Tel. (213) 482 5050, Fax. (213) 482 9850.

California Overseas Bank, 3701 Wilshire Blvd, Los Angeles CA 90010, Tel. (213) 736 9400, Fax. (213) 383 6477.

Cathay Bank, 777 N Broadway, Los Angeles CA 90012, Tel. (231) 625 4700.

Dai-Ichi Kangyo Bank, 770 Wilshire Blvd, Los Angeles CA 90071, Tel (213) 489 1000, Fax. (213) 622 8975.

First Interstate Bank of California, 707 Wilshire Blvd, Los Angeles CA 90017, Tel. (213) 239 4000.

First Los Angeles Bank, 2049 Century Park E, 36th Floor, Los Angeles CA 90067, Tel. (213) 557 1211,
Fax. (213) 556 1205.

General Bank, 210 S. Figueroa Street, Los Angeles CA 90012, Tel. (213) 972 4163, Fax. (213) 680 3130.

Mercantile National Bank, 1840 Century Park E, Los Angeles CA 90067, Tel. (213) 277 2265,
Fax. (213) 201 0862.

Mitsubishi Bank of California, 800 Wilshire Blvd, Los Angeles CA 90017, Tel. (213) 621 1200,
Fax. (213) 613 1136.

Mitsui Manufacturers Bank Los Angeles, 515 S. Figueroa, Los Angeles CA 90071, Tel. (213) 485 0331,
Fax. (213) 623 3935.

Business Guide

L.A at Dusk

Security Pacific National Bank, 333 Hope Street, Los Angeles CA 90071, Tel. (213) 345 6211, Fax. (213) 625 0809.

Tokai Bank of California, 534 W 6th Street, Los Angeles CA 90014, Tel. (213) 972 0200, Fax. (213) 972 0154.

Union Bank, 445 S. Figueroa Street, Los Angeles CA 90071, Tel. (213) 236 5000.

Business Guide

Business Publications

Business Week, 3333 Wilshire Blvd, Suite 407, Los Angeles CA 90010 Tel.(213) 487 1160.

California Business, 4221 Wilshire Blvd, Suite 400, Los Angeles
CA 90010, Tel.(213) 937 5820.

Forbes, 12233 W. Olympic Blvd, Suite 370, Los Angeles CA 90064 Tel.(213) 820 1140.

Los Angeles Business Journal, 3345 Wilshire Blvd, Suite 20
Los Angeles CA 90010, Tel.(213) 385 9050.

Wall Street Journal, 514 Shatto Place, Los Angeles CA 90020
Tel.(213) 658 6464.

Chamber of Commerce

Catalina Island Chamber of Commerce, Green Pier, Avalon CA 90740
Tel.(213) 510 1520.

Hollywood Chamber of Commerce, 6255 Sunset Blvd, Hollywood CA 90028
Tel.(213) 469 8311.

Los Angeles Area Chamber of Commerce,
404 South Bixel Street
Los Angeles CA 90051, Tel.(213) 482 1311.

Oceanside Chamber of Commerce, 928 North Hill Street
Oceanside CA 92504, Tel.(619) 721 1101.

Ridgecrest Chamber of Commerce,
301-A South China Lake Blvd
Ridgecrest CA 93555, Tel.(619) 375 8331.

Santa Barbara Conference and Visitors Bureau, 222 E Anapamu Street
Santa Barbara CA93101, Tel.(805) 966 9222.

Los Angeles Convention and Visitors Bureau,
695 Figueroa Street
Los Angeles CA 90017, Tel.(213) 689 8822.

Business Guide

Convention Facilities

The expanded **Los Angeles Convention Centre** is one of the largest and finest convention and exhibition centre in the world.

The complex offers 685,000 square feet of exhibit area, 65 meeting rooms inclusive of a 26,500 square foot special events hall, lobbies, restaurants and over 6,000 parking spaces plus shuttle-bus and taxi drop-off areas.

The South Hall provides 350,000 square feet of exhibit space and with the two moveable soundproof partitions can accommodate one large show or sub-divide into two or three halls to host simultaneously smaller events.

Concourse hall, is 26,500 square feet for special events, small exhibits a general session or a banquet for over 1,700, or eight different meetings. It occupies 58 acres and is conveniently located close to the Interstate Freeway System and the Downtown hotel community.

For information on events call the Visitors Convention Bureau Tel.(213) 689 8822.

Business Guide

Credit Cards

All major credit cards are accepted in the United States, American Express (AE), Master Card (MC), Visa (VI), Diner's Club (DC) and Carte Blanche (CB). Some companies also accept the Discover Card and Japan Credit Bureau. Telephone numbers and addresses can be found in the local telephone books.

Translators and Interpreters

These are easily available through your hotel reception or your tour operator.

Fax and Secretarial Services

The majority of hotels provide the above services but there are numerous business bureaus available through the Yellow Pages telephone book.

Major Airlines

Aerolineous Argentina, Tel: (213) 683-1070
Air Canada, Tel: (800) 422-6232
All Nippon Airway, Tel: (213) 629-1500
American Airlines, Tel: (213) 932-2421
Delta Airlines Inc, Tel: (213) 736 1231
Japan Airlines, Tel: (213) 620 9580
Scandinavian Airlines, Tel: (213) 652 8612
Varig Brazilian Airlines, Tel: (800) 468 2744
Pan Am, Tel: (800) 221 1111
Philippine Airlines, Tel: (800) 435 9725
Quantas, Tel: (800) 622 0850
Singapore Airlines, Tel: (213) 655 9270
South African Airways, Tel: (800) 722 9675
Swissair, Tel: (213) 410 9340
Tahi Airways, Tel: (800) 426 5204
TWA, Tel: (213) 484 9319
KLM, Tel: (213) 776 6300
Alitalia, Tel: (800) 223 5730
British Caledonian, Tel: (800) 231 0270
UTA French Airlines, Tel: (213) 649 2222
JAT, Yugoslav Airlines, Tel: (213) 388 0379
TACA Airlines, Tel: (800) 535 8780

Business Guide

OREGON
River
Pit
Kalmath
River
Eureka
Shasta Lake
Redding
Red Bluff
Eel
River
Coast
Ranges
Sacramento
R
Lake
Oroville
Reno
SIERRA
Lake
Tahoe
Lake Tahoe
Ukiah
Clear
Lake
Cache
Ck
Russian
Santa Rosa
Sacramento
CALIFORNIA
Richmond
Stockton
SAN FRANCISCO
Oakland
San
Joaquin
River
Fremont
San Jose
Atwater
Fresno
Salinas
Monterey
Coast
Ranges
Salinas
River
PACIFIC
OCEAN
Santa Maria
Santa
Barbara
CHANNEL

LEGEND

═══	Main Road
───	Railway
✈	International Airport
✈	Airport

0 50 100
Kilometres

IDAHO
NEVADA
UTAH
Mono Lake
Death Valley
Las Vagas
Hoover Dam
Colorado River
ARIZONA
Kern River
Bakersfield
Barstow
MOJAVE DESERT
Ventura
Los Angeles
San Bernadino
Santa Monica
Riverside
Long Beach
Santa Ana
ISLANDS
Gulf of Santa Catalina
Salton Sea
San Diego
MEXICO

Alphabetical Index

A

A-Z Summary 136
Advance Planning 139
Ahmanson Theatre 65
American Indians 19
Anaheim 111
Angelino Heights 67
Angelus Temple 67
Art 34
Art Galleries 142
Asians 20
Avenue of the Stars 97
Avila Abode 58

B

Banks 186
Beaches 101
Bel Air 96
Berwin Entertainment Centre 75
Beverly Hills 91
Beverly Hills Hotel 92
Beverly Hills Post Office 92
Biltmore Hotel 62
Blacks 23
Bonaventure Hotel 64
Brentwood 101
Bunker Hill 64
Business Briefing 185
Business Publications 188
Business guide 185

C

Capistrano 112
Capitol Records 78
Casinos and Card Clubs 143
Century City 97
Century Plaza Towers 97
Chamber of Commerce 188
Chateu Marmont 83
Children's Entertainment 143
Chinatown 60
Chinese 20
Chumash 19

Cinema 143
Cinerama Dome Theatre 75
City Hall 63
City of Angeles 9
Climate 12
Commerce 17
Concerts 146
Concessions
    for all Travellers 140
Consulates 152
Convention Facilities 189
Credit Cards 190
Crime 155
Cruises 177
Crystal Cathedral 111
Cuisine 37
Currency 141, 185
Customs 140

D

Dance 33
Death 153
Design 35
Dinner Theatres 168
Disabled people
    Information 154
Disneyland 108
Dodger Stadium 68
Downtown 57
Dust Bowlers 46

E

Early Settlement 40
Echo Park 67
Education 16
El Pueblo 57
El Pueblo de la Reina
    de Los Angeles 43
Electricity 142
Elysian Park 68
Ennis-Brown House 70
Entertainment 142
Entry Regulations 139
European Settlement 42
Exposition Park 66

Index

F

Fairfax District 87
Farmer's Market 88
Festivals 144
Flora and Fauna 14

G

Gardens of the Clear Stream 61
Garment District 63
Geology and Geography 11
Getting Around L.A 148
Getting Outside L.A 151
Getting to Los Angeles 141
Government 15
Gower Gulch 74
Grand Central Market 62
Greaser Law 44
Griffith Park 69

H

Help 151
Hispanics 24
Historical/Cultural Dates 38
Hollywood 60
Hollywood Bowl 82
Hollywood Bowl 32
Hollywood Sign 71
Hollywood Wax Museum 80
Hollywood and Vine 76
Hotels 121

I

Index 194
Industry 17

J

J Paul Getty Museum 106
Japanese 22
Justice 16

K

KCET Studio 69
KTLA Studios 74
Knott's Berry Farm 110

Koreans 22
Koreatown 89

L

L.A Ballet 33
L.A Philharmonic Orchestra 32
La Brea Tar Pits 90
Laguna Beach 111
Language 28
Libraries 157
Literature 29
Little Tokyo 60
Live Animals 140
Los Angeles 55
Los Feliz 70
Lost Property 154
Lower Downtown 62

M

Macarthur Park 89
Magic Castle 81
Major Airlines 190
Malibu 107
Mann's Chinese Theatre 80
Marina Del Rey 104
Mark Taper Forum 65
Medical Emergencies 153
Meeting People 26
Melrose Avenue 86
Memorial Coliseum 66
Mestizos 24
Metric System 178
Miracle Mile 90
Motoring 155
Movies 34
Muscle Beach 103
Music 32, 146
Music Centre 65
Mythology 37

N

Nearby Districts 108
New Era 44
Newport Beach 111
Nightclubs 158
Nightlife 158
Norton Simon Museum 114

Index

O

Observatory and Planetarium 70
Olvera Street 57
Orange County 108
Orchestras 146

P

Pacific Asian Museum 114
Pacific Islanders 23
Pacific Palisades 105
Pan Pacific Auditorium 88
Pantages Theatre 77
Parks with Sports Facilities 175
Pasadena 113
Pasadena Playhouse 115
People 18
Pershing Square 62
Plants 140
Police Emergencies 153
Post Office 157
Pre-History 38
Public Holidays 145

R

Radio/Television 148
Recreation 35
Religion 17
Religious 158
Rental Cars 156
Replacement of Certain Items 154
Restaurants 158-161
Rock Row 84
Rodeo Drive 95
Roxy 84

S

San Fernando Valley 73
San Fernando Valley 112
Santa Monica 101
Secretarial Services 190
Shopping Hours 171
Shopping Plazas and Malls 169
Shoshome 19
Silverlake 70
Sport 35
Sporting Complexes 172
Sports 172
Sunset Strip 82
Super Tram 72

T

Telephones/Telegraphs 176
Television 34
Temecula 112
Thais 23
Theatre 146
Theatre 31
Time 177
Tipping 176
Tourism 48
Tourist Services 178
Tours 177
Town of the Queen of the Angeles 43
Translators/Interpreters 190
Travel Town 71

U

Union Station 58
Univ. of Southern California 66
Universal Studios 71
Upper Downtown 64

V

Venice Beach 102
Vietnamese 23
Village Theatre 100

W

Walk of Fame 78
Westwood Village 98
Whites 25
Wilshire Boulevard 89

Y

Yamashimo 80

Z

Zoo 71

Notes

Notes

Notes